Engaging Learners
Through Artmaking

Choice-Based Art Education
in the Classroom

Engaging Learners Through Artmaking

Choice-Based Art Education in the Classroom

KATHERINE M. DOUGLAS
DIANE B. JAQUITH

Foreword by George Szekely
Preface by John V. Crowe

TEACHERS COLLEGE PRESS

TEACHERS COLLEGE | COLUMBIA UNIVERSITY
NEW YORK AND LONDON

Published by Teachers College Press, 1234 Amsterdam Avenue, New York, NY 10027

Library of Congress Cataloging-in-Publication Data

Douglas, Katherine M.
    Engaging learners through artmaking : choice-based art education in the classroom / Katherine M. Douglas, Diane B. Jaquith ; foreword by George Szekely ; preface by John V. Crowe.
        p.   cm.
    Includes bibliographical references and index.
    ISBN 978-0-8077-4976-0 (pbk. : alk. paper)
1. Art—Study and teaching (Elementary) 2. Art—Study and teaching (Secondary) I. Jaquith, Diane B. II. Title.
    N350.D6 2009
    372.5'044—dc22   2009000546

ISBN: 978-0-8077-4976-0 (paperback)

Printed on acid-free paper
Manufactured in the United States of America
16   8 7 6

This book is dedicated to Pauline Joseph, whose wisdom, wit, and conviction in honoring the child as artist shape the foundation of our pedagogy.

Contents

Foreword

After a candy-pile night of trick-or-treating, the butterfly closed up her wings and retired to examine her bounty. Dumping the contents of the paper jack-o-lantern on the kitchen table, my granddaughter smiled and went to work. During the course of the evening, Emilie built candy towers, chocolate cars, and a fancy version of her name using lollipops as big red dots. The candy artist refueled with treats, proceeding even more energetically to find new possibilities in her palette.

To function as an artist, a child requires a canvas—in this case the kitchen table, and the recognition that candy is an art supply. With the confidence of an expert player who knows that art supplies lie everywhere, the young artist sets out to explore. The information adults can teach children about art is as vast as the history of art itself, yet it is children's artistic behaviors that allow them to spend hours of intense concentration on independent artmaking.

This book suggests the essence of art teaching, which is to inquire the following: What do we need to provide young artists that will allow them to take full advantage of their artistic behavior? The authors describe what we can make available in school and at home, so that children can continue to function as artists. A guiding light to teaching art is looking at children engaged in playful and creative activities. In Halloween art, we see the importance of maintaining play and independence, so that children have the self-confidence to discover art and act on their ideas. An art curriculum that provides for basic artistic behaviors will sustain an artist and art connoisseur for life.

When teachers construct art curriculums and approaches to teaching art to children, they often reach into a bag of tricks—consulting other adults about what is good for children and what aspects of adult art children should study. Teaching adult art to children neglects the one certainty in the art world: change. If you don't follow the art world for a moment, there will be hundreds of new artists and art trends passing by. There will always be new materials, media, and techniques to consider. Perhaps the fundamental question for all art teachers to consider is one that asks, "What is timeless in art?" Besides the surface articulations of space, shape, and "beauty," what is more steadfast and timeless than the antiquities of artistic standards? It is emotion that compels creation and includes fun and play— it is a child's pure artistic behavior. What art teachers should ask is, what is timeless in art? The answer is children's artistic behavior. Yet the appreciation of adult art and techniques was not the essence of our Halloween evening. It was the artistic playing of a young artist, sleeping with an old slide box that has a tastefully glued, candy-furnished home inside.

When the slide box is transported to art class the next day, it is to raise awareness of the uniqueness of children's art. A timeless art curriculum includes the appreciation of children's artistic behaviors. An art class is a place where children's collections, finds, and ideas are the stars, and supportive adults treat their art seriously. The goal of art teaching is to recognize the child-artist, who comes to the art class with rich resumes and pockets filled with collections. An art class is providing the time and opportunity for children to share ideas and act on their plans.

The authors and I have supported each other's work in art education for more than a decade. We believe in a curriculum that enlivens playful hands and promotes freely moving bodies in an art class and that art teaching has to engage children in independent artmaking. We know that children's artistic behaviors exist in their confidence as "idea people," seeing themselves as artists with many good ideas. We believe in the power of children as players, inventors, and futurists.

This book contains some of the most important wisdom to be shared with art teachers, who are entrusted with supporting the creative life of young artists like Emilie. The writing represents experienced voices that have spent their careers setting up studios as safe places for students to be creative in school. The authors share their most valuable insights of observing, supporting and modeling artistic behaviors in teaching art to children.

—*George Szekeley*

man, & Stuhr, 1996). In addition, the practice certainly teaches students "to construct meaning in works of art by attending to formal qualities, artist's intention/context, and personal experience" (Hutchens & Suggs, 1997, p. 151) and embraces formal art principles along with postmodern versions as described by Gude (2004). Choice-based art education fits the description of a postmodern, kaleidoscope curriculum; "the designs [are] constantly changing and becoming something new, and yet all of them remain interrelated." (Slattery, 1995, p. 257) In the end, Douglas and Jaquith's book offers a call to action and to hope, one that Smith (1996, p. 218) hadn't seen in what he has referred to as his "so often dark study" of art education history.

From my current overview as art education professor now removed from daily contact with K–12 students, I am deeply moved by the promise of teaching for artistic behavior in all its variations. One spectacular reminder was TAB's first national exhibition held at Massachusetts College of Art and Design's Arnheim Gallery during the National Art Education Association's Boston conference in March 2005. This exhibit is featured in Plate P.1. This landmark exhibition demonstrated the absolute antithesis of Arthur Efland's (1976) "school art style" and Peter Smith's (1995) "irrelevant" art. The wide range of work demonstrated the variety of students' concerns both profound and trivial: touching tributes to WWII grandfather veterans, serial goldfish deaths, a future entrepreneur's vision of a flower shop, a visual battle of "dizzy" and "queezy" drawings, and a twig zoo. The content demonstrated in these students' artworks was genuine and accomplished, and supported the vision of the arts as a vital life force. In *Engaging Learners Through Art-making: Choice-Based Art Education in the Classroom*, Douglas and Jaquith describe a variety of practices which promise to renew our faith in the power of truly creative endeavors.

—*John V. Crowe*

Preface

Engaging Learners Through Artmaking: Choice-Based Art Education in the Classroom connects choice-based practices with the philosophy of teaching for artistic behavior. This pedagogy is developed by and for practicing art teachers and has grown from deep reflection, dedication, vision, collegial relationships, and action research over many years. The true collaborative nature of this approach includes the creation of this book. Authors Kathy Douglas and Diane Jaquith have worked tirelessly since the late 1990s to establish and maintain a vibrant choice-based teacher network. This grass-roots organization serves to support, mentor, and give voice to practicing art teachers. Consistent with their classroom pedagogy, Douglas and Jaquith have invested their energy in designing an evolving framework for choice-based teaching and learning that supports emergent professional development. The concept sustains peer mentoring and collaborating, numerous local and national conference presentations and exhibitions, weekend and summer retreats, and impressive Internet sites. Teaching for artistic behavior has now developed into a vital national professional learning community.

Although the extensive network described above is relatively recent, choice-based art education's roots go back to the early 1970s. Out of the pure necessity of providing authentic art experiences, teachers were inspired to offer real choices to students—it was simply common sense to them. They were inspired by their own studio experiences, collaborations with artist friends, and deep thinking about true creative behavior. They designed and refined curricula and classrooms to provide learners with rich studio environments for them to pursue teacher-demonstrated artmaking practices or the students' own independent or collaborative interests.

Over the years, increasingly formal associations resulted in the founding of the Teaching for Artistic Behavior (TAB) organization in 2001. This national presence has engaged numerous new and veteran educators and continues to attract solo teachers who have established and run similar programs, some for decades. TAB's existence is enabled by the Internet and the expert caretaking by Douglas and Jaquith. Although supported by higher education institutions (Brown University, Massachusetts College of Art and Design, and Bridgewater State College), TAB remains an independent movement firmly planted in classroom practice.

My own practice of choice-based teaching commenced when, as a teacher with 15 years of high school experience, I returned to teach Grades 1–6 in a lab school. My strict Lowenfeld education, which had served me so well in my earlier elementary art teaching career, seemed inadequate upon my return from the secondary level. First of all, Lowenfeld's motivational model on a single topic was mismatched to my classes of wide academic diversity and even wider spans of interests. Children's worlds, including school life, had changed over 15 years. With heterogeneous grouping and inclusion of special needs students, one single lesson no longer fit all. Also, my own secondary school practice of talking to students in an intimate, artist-to-artist manner was sacrificed in my teacher-centered mode. Overall, I was bored with my own ability to make a single lesson work and haunted by using a single source of motivation. Although I did not label them as such at the time, the "Eight Studio Habits of Mind" (Hetland, Winner, Veenema, & Sheridan, 2007, p. 6) so present in my high school teaching experience were diminished in my K–6 teacher-centered approach. After talking with Kathy Douglas, I established my own variations of choice-based teaching that resulted in a personal midcareer renaissance. Giving up the control and the teacher drama of my Lowenfeld-based practice allowed me to relate to students in a mutually engaged manner that was surprising, improvisational, and both intellectually and expressively rich. If one asks, "Who is engaging and persisting?" and "Who is doing the envisioning?" (Hetland et al., 2007) and the honest answer is the teacher, a shake-up is needed.

The success of teaching for artistic behavior lies in its flexibility and inclusiveness. It is truly an open system which has been implemented in a variety of settings and hybridized with art education traditions of direct instruction, demonstrations, problem posing, studio practices, and assessment. For example, I can picture teachers using a Lowenfeld-like motivation, gathering students who do not have studio plans for the day and offering it as an inspirational option.

In the context of art education history, choice-based art education resolves the conflict between teaching for content and encouraging self-expression described by Efland (1990) and bridges the gulf between the art world and the world of school art described by Smith (1996). This concept offers one way of adapting essentialist and reconstructive models of art education (Clark, 1996). Teaching for artistic behavior fits the description of postmodern art and art education as a form of cultural production and reproduction capable of dissolving boundaries; exploring nonlinear progression; embracing the realism of society and culture; expanding notions of power, beauty, and connoisseurship; and integrating the past and present (Efland, Freed-

Acknowledgments

This book results from the creativity, generosity, and enthusiasm of those who have inspired us, taught us, and supported us. We are extremely appreciative of the exceptional efforts of John Crowe and Nan Hathaway, who read drafts with a sharp eye and held us accountable for staying true to our vision. We thank Pauline Joseph and George Szekely, who have always believed in the child as the artist; and the writers and collaborators for this book: Renee Brannigan, Clark Fralick, Clyde Gaw, Laurie Jakubiak, Bonnie Muir, Judy Decker, and the seven hundred members of the Teaching for Artistic Behavior listserv.

We thank our readers, who provided valuable comments, insights, and questions: Georgia Smith, Wendy Protheroe, and Candace Wood; David Frazer of RISD, whose vision of a studio classroom 35 years ago inspired Kathy; school principals George Frye and Cindy Bencal, whose trust and support enabled Kathy and Diane to navigate a less traveled path in education.

We thank our editors, Adee Braun and Lori Tate, and the Teachers College Press production team for guiding us through the publication process; and Mary DePalma for her advice on legal matters.

We thank our families for their constant support, patience, and humor throughout this enormous project. Carl, Becca, Katie, and Andy; Maurice, Lia, and Luke, we thank you from the bottom of our collective hearts.

Choice-based educators are in the presence of the world's best teachers every day—their students. The joy of our careers has been to watch and learn from the curiosity and energy of children.

Introducing Choice-Based Art Education

The Spirit of Artistic Behavior

> *Art teaching has yet to be invented.*
> (Szekely, 1988)

Alert and eager to get started with their artwork, third graders focus on their teacher's opening message. Imagine that among the 26 seated children are 8-year-old versions of painter Helen Frankenthaler, architect I. M. Pei, potter Maria Martinez, collage artist Romare Beardon, photographer Ansel Adams, and architect-sculptor Maya Lin. Imagine also that this class contains a young Marie Curie, Steve Jobs, and Maya Angelou. This group of unique individuals is representative of the diversity of students found in elementary schools. What single lesson could this art teacher deliver to meet the needs of these varied learners?

The simple answer is that there is no one lesson and no one way to provide instruction in visual art that will satisfy all the curiosities, interests, and personalities in a classroom of learners. Students need to learn about materials and techniques, concepts and art history; teachers need to connect the child's world to the curriculum. This requires rethinking the art program. Imagine the following:

- Curriculum that emerges out of student-directed learning rather than explicit directions, eliminating the endless search for new lesson plans
- Curriculum flexible enough to meet the unique needs of individuals and classes while addressing visual arts standards
- Motivated students who bring their art ideas to class and engage in meaningful work
- Students starting without your assistance, setting up materials, and putting them away when they are finished

- Knowing your students through the content of their artwork
- Learners successfully forming their own collaborative groups, coaching peers, and assisting with classmates' challenges
- Not having to modify lessons for challenged learners
- Needing only enough materials for a few students at a time in each center
- Children helping to stock the art room with objects they collect
- Being able to work and converse alongside a small group of invested students
- Assessing what an individual really knows and can do by their artistic behaviors
- Children in Grades K–8 conducting independent studies, manageable even with 700 students
- Every day bringing unexpected and amazing discoveries

Where else in the school day can children consistently engage in work that has personal relevance, utilizes higher order thinking skills, and is exciting for both student and teacher? Teaching for artistic behavior offers educators and learners a structure for authentic learning while making art.

By celebrating artistic behaviors and providing circumstances for their continued development, teachers and parents can encourage children to build confidence as artists. By respecting the child as artist, the art teacher sets the stage for authentic creative exploration. Increased confidence leads to actions, which in turn stimulate initiative. Repeated over time, these spiraling actions result in artistic growth.

ARTISTIC BEHAVIORS

Creative processes unique to each artist spring from individual experiences, knowledge, skills, and perspective. *Process*, an umbrella term referring to myriad ways in which an artist works, becomes more clearly defined through repeated actions. Often fluid and flexible, artistic process may constantly redefine itself or may gradually settle into routines. Activities that inform and sustain creative process are *artistic behaviors*. Because artistic behaviors are so numerous and varied, there is no direct way to teach them; instead we teach *for* artistic behavior. These behaviors support artistic inquiry and self-driven activities for individuals during and outside of art class. Offering instruction in materials and techniques and providing resources, time, and space are ways that art educators can support and encourage students as they develop their own creative process. By setting up proper circumstances, teachers create opportunities for a variety of artistic behaviors to emerge and flourish.

To determine the circumstances under which artmaking will thrive, teachers need first to identify what it is that artists do, and then ask how to create a learning environment where these types of behaviors can be supported. These are some ways that adult artists work:

- Play with materials
- Dream and mentally plan
- Conceive and expand ideas for artmaking
- Risk false starts, abandon failed attempts
- Utilize materials in traditional and idiosyncratic ways
- Combine materials and genres (e.g., sculpture with painting)
- Complete several pieces in a very short time or work for weeks on one piece
- Pursue multiple works at the same time
- Follow a particular line of thinking over time, sometimes repeating a series of similar works
- Accept mistakes as the springboard for new directions
- Comment on one's life, beliefs, popular culture, politics, and history

We have collaborated with a group of choice-based art teachers to develop an elemental list of some artistic behaviors (see Sidebar I.1).

CHOICE-BASED ART EDUCATION

In traditional school art programs, students develop skills in a range of media, experience techniques carefully researched and presented by their art teacher, and learn about featured artists and movements. It is unlikely that students will become knowledgeable about their *own* artistry unless they have the means to self-direct their work throughout the year. Control must pass from teacher to student so they can pursue independent work in a carefully planned learning environment. Studio centers, similar to classroom learning centers, provide access to multiple choices in the art classroom. It is difficult to find a phrase that describes the complexity and subtlety of teaching for artistic behavior. We call this learner-centered practice *choice-based art education* and believe it offers students authentic experiences for artmaking by providing real choices.

Choice-based art education provides for the development of artistic behaviors by enabling students to discover what it means to be an artist through the *authentic* creation of artwork. The ability to make one's own choices and decisions regarding one's work is a contributing factor for creativity (Ama-

Sidebar I.1. Artistic Behaviors

This list is the result of action research generated by a group of choice-based art teachers in the summer of 2008 and is in no way an exhaustive list. In the true nature of being open to possibilities, there are infinite variations for artistic behaviors yet to be discovered.

Problem Finding

- Identify questions
- Research
- Visualize possibilities
- Think divergently

Problem Solving

- Revise, refine, or reinvent ideas
- Intuit
- Infer and understand
- Ponder

Constructing Knowledge

- Apply concepts to work
- Synthesize understandings in new situations

Experimenting

- Play
- Improvise
- Explore media
- Innovate

Working Habits

- Plan and sketch
- Pace
- Persevere
- Engage
- Set goals
- Collaborate or not
- Discuss
- Collect objects, data, materials
- Organize
- Take risks

- Practice and repeat skills and techniques
- Rework mistakes
- Work in a series or not

Representing

- Observe
- Compose
- Express
- Communicate ideas visually
- Represent a point of view
- Develop style

Reflecting

- Perceive
- Question
- Interpret
- Assess
- Critique self and others
- Apply understandings
- Find meaning

Connecting

- Connect with other disciplines
- Make associations
- Examine artwork
- Respond to visual culture
- Develop empathy

Valuing

- Embrace freedom
- Appreciate ambiguity
- Open up to possibilities
- Make choices

bile, 1996; Fasko, 2006; Runco, 2006). The capacity to make choices and work independently must be learned with lots of practice and support from the teacher (Tomlinson, 1999). A choice-based learning environment provides space, time, varied materials and instruction, and a climate that is conducive to independent work and the development of artistic behaviors. The classroom space is organized around studio centers complete with materials, tools, and resources necessary for each medium. Classes are carefully planned to maximize students' time in these studio centers. Students determine their own pace, based on the work they choose. Materials are accessible and plentiful. Instruction comes in multiple forms: whole group, small group, individual, peer, and collaborative, as well as indirectly from visual references.

Choice-based art education is nurtured by the same practices that are proven effective in general education. Teachers map and differentiate this curriculum, align it with visual arts standards, and utilize multiple formative assessments to measure growth. The constructivist setting in the choice-based art room promotes child-centered learning by meeting students at their own developmental levels. Some students form collaborative groups naturally while others prefer independent work. The teacher conducts action research formally and informally to investigate methods to improve student learning. With teaching and learning structures firmly embedded, the art classroom becomes a highly functioning public studio.

The main focus of teaching for artistic behavior is to facilitate and encourage the generation of art ideas. Translating ideas to visual form can be both intellectual and visceral. Practice is necessary to acquire facility in expressing ideas, a central skill vital to all disciplines. When students interact with studio centers and with one another, the unique learning environment fosters creative thinking. Our inquiry over the past 35 years indicates significant outcomes for art education and is supported in research by Hetland et al. (2007):

> Our aim is to provide strong evidence that the real curriculum in the visual arts extends far beyond the teaching of technique, and to demonstrate that such teaching engenders the development of serious thinking dispositions that are valued both within and beyond the arts. (p. vii)

It is in the very spirit of artistic behavior that we plan, organize, and run our choice-based art programs. Young artists need to be given freedom to follow their ideas and to learn by taking risks. They need to know that their teachers trust them to make good choices. Choice-based art teachers regard students as artists, giving them full ownership of their artwork. If we wish for our students to do the work of artists, we must offer them the opportunity to behave as artists, think as artists, and perform as artists. If not in our classrooms, then where?

Practice-Based Theory

Learner engagement surfaces and grows through opportunities to connect students' work to their unique lives. Intrinsic motivation drives students in choice-based classrooms to explore their personal interests and curiosities at their own pace, while their classmates engage in similar pursuits with the same or different media. This constructivist and standards-based approach is possible even with large class size and low budgets. Part I focuses on instruction, assessment, and management practices of choice-based art programs. Emphasis is placed on artistic process with three essential goals: student independence, acquisition of artistic behaviors, and the generation of ideas. As control gradually shifts from teacher to child, responsibility for learning transfers to the student. Efficient structures for the arrangement of time, space, and materials support differentiated instruction for all learners.

Instruction varies from whole and small group demonstrations to individual and peer coaching. Maintaining high expectations for all students requires frequent monitoring of student understandings. Some schools will present challenges to art instruction; even in difficult circumstances choice-based instruction and assessment strategies offer effective solutions. Part I concludes with the topic of exhibits, as a means to highlight student achievements and celebrate artistic behaviors.

For those familiar with choice-based practices, Part I will reinforce the philosophy of teaching for artistic behavior. Teachers new to this pedagogy will discover the rationale and framework for authentic art education through teaching for artistic behavior.

CHAPTER 1

Defining Teaching for Artistic Behavior

The Four Practices

I am me. I may look like you, but if you take a closer look you will realize that I am nothing like you at all. I am very different. I see things through a completely different perspective because in my life I had experiences that you didn't have, and I had feelings you didn't have, and I've lived places and seen places and experienced life from a completely different point of view than you have. I may be wearing the same shoes and the same haircut, but that gives you no right to have any preconceived notions about what I am or who I am.
(Haring, 1996, p. 12)

By teaching for artistic behavior, educators facilitate authentic choices for students and honor their ideas for artmaking. This is the core of our pedagogy. In a choice-based art program, teachers are arranging circumstances for the development of artistic behaviors through demonstrations and carefully planned studio centers. Four practices define the educational scope: personal, pedagogical, classroom, and assessment. These practices form the structure of choice-based art education and are described in this chapter.

PRACTICE ONE: STUDENTS AS ARTISTS

Choice-based art education regards students as artists and offers students real choices for responding to their own ideas and interests through artmaking.
(Douglas, Crowe, Jaquith, & Brannigan, 2002)

Students in Control

The student is the artist. This powerful statement insures that students will have control over their subject matter, materials, and approach. Painter Keith Haring's statement above is testimony to the power of personal experience. Art that is created from the meaningful context of young artists' lives enhances relevancy and authenticity. Students who maintain control over their work are invested and have incentives to take risks. Resulting artwork is often powerful and profound.

Real Choices

Choice practice allows teachers and students to value authentic learning processes and intrinsic motivation. In a fully operating choice program, students have access to all materials in every studio center during every art class. The predictability of studio centers facilitates student planning, discovering, and collecting materials. Students work from their strengths and learn at an individual pace. Routines are quickly internalized. Scribbling, experimentation, and discovery learning are necessary opportunities for beginners. These forms of play, vital to creativity, lead to divergent thinking and generation of ideas (Runco, 2007), which may appear in current work or resurface months later in different artwork. Students share their discoveries with classmates, sometimes resulting in artmaking trends. Self-selected teams work collaboratively while others pursue their ideas independently. Some students take home finished work each week; other classmates might rehearse for many weeks prior to completing an artwork acceptable to them. Learners who return often to the same studio center construct deep understandings through trial and error. Identifying one's preferred working style is one of many cognitive behaviors supported by choice-based education. Teachers learn to recognize stages of development at each studio center and support learning within each particular medium.

PRACTICE TWO: PEDAGOGY

Choice-based art education supports multiple modes of learning and teaching.
(Douglas et al., 2002)

Differentiation permeates the learning environment with multiple forms of instruction throughout the class period. Choice-based teachers employ varied teaching and learning strategies to meet diverse students' needs. Students demonstrate a readiness to learn, and teachers respond with instruction to meet that readiness.

Teacher Roles

Choice-based teaching comes in many forms: direct and indirect (through visuals and references), whole-group demonstrations and discussions, small groups with students who choose a particular exploration, and one-to-one interactions. These multiple approaches are possible because student independence is encouraged. Teacher roles include demonstrating, modeling, facilitating, coaching, providing curriculum content, and altering that content as a result of observations made in class. The teacher also ensures accessibility of art materials, tools, and visual references for independent learning through student-directed experiences. Beghetto & Plucker (2006), Brooks & Brooks (1993), and Duckworth (1996) support constructivist theory, which states that learners build upon their knowledge by connecting new experiences to existing understandings. Students select their level of challenge, and teachers help them adjust as needed, pairing students' objectives with their skills (Saphier & Gower, 1997). Getting to know students through their particular work habits and interests (as shown in their artwork) enables the teacher to differentiate instruction for individual needs (Tomlinson, 1999). Finding a balance between direct teaching and stepping back allows students more autonomy, as shown in Figure 1.1.

Student Roles

When we teach for artistic behavior, children are constantly engaged in authentic learning experiences where they must apply their knowledge to their work. When students self-direct, they build understandings through inquiry and problem solving. In multiple studio centers around the classroom, learners provide much of the instruction. Students who work in one medium over time serve as peer coaches, expanding their own knowledge in the process. Peer coaching is encouraged and, in fact, is necessary to maintain a highly active learning environment. Many students get ideas and observe techniques by watching their classmates at work. Discoveries are shared; newly mixed colors, kinetic sculptures, and first stitches are all cause for celebration. Students form cooperative groups in an organic manner to expand their artmaking. Individual pursuits and group collaborations are equally honored. In these ways a great deal of information is transmitted from student to student. An 8-year-old, Sean, describes a spontaneous group painting experience:

> Me and Dean started this. Sarah overheard us. Then she started helping. Dean decided that it would be the "Ocean Rainbow Sunset." We painted the rainbow. Sarah mostly mixed the colors. We couldn't say no to her! Sarah stopped her own painting to help us. Sarah said, "I am on vacation."

While teachers organize and supply studio centers, it is the responsibility of students to maintain these centers. Routines for setting up and cleaning

FIGURE 1.1. Continuum of Choice-Based Teaching and Learning

Explicit Curriculum Teacher-Directed	←——→	Emergent Curriculum Student-Directed
No Choice	*Modified Choice*	*Full Choice*
• Teacher assigns content and media	• Teacher chooses content, student chooses media *or* • Student chooses content, teacher chooses media	• Students are problem finders and problem solvers • Students select content and media all of the time
	• Teacher is flexible with curriculum in response to student interests and needs	• Students have full ownership of process, direction, outcomes

up workspaces are an important part of classroom management. Students inform their teachers when issues arise with materials, tools, and resources. When students take full ownership of their work, they have strong incentive to care for their favorite studio centers.

Visual References

References are plentiful in the choice-based art room. The worlds of art, nature and history are available to students who find connections to their work through reproductions, books, Web sites, and multimedia materials. Because individual students' directions are recognized, teachers are able to locate resources in support of their interests and concerns. In Plate 1.1, a student works on a drawing using visual references. This emergent curriculum fosters a natural learning process where the unique needs of a particular class, group, or individual can be met.

PRACTICE THREE: CLASSROOM CONTEXT

*Choice-based art education provides resources and opportunities to construct
knowledge and meaning in the process of making art.*
(Douglas et al., 2002)

The ideal learning environment for student-driven artmaking requires the efficient structure of time, careful arrangement of space, and thoughtful choice of materials. Good classroom management allows teachers to respond in a timely manner to student needs. Predictability of studio centers is central to the effectiveness of choice-based teaching and learning, and enables students to plan ahead for their art class.

Structuring Time

Whole-group demonstrations at the beginning of each class are carefully planned to be brief. The purpose of the demo is for students to receive exposure to varied art concepts over the course of the school year. Learners may choose to try something new every week or to continue working on one piece for an extended period of time. Studio work takes up the majority of the period. Individual class dynamics determine how much time is required for cleanup and sharing at the end of art class.

Arranging Space

Classrooms are arranged to accommodate an enormous number of resources and materials and to facilitate both group and independent work. Patterns of use at each center emerge when students become familiar with the arrangements. Teacher observations lead to adjustments that allow better functioning of the centers. Including students in decisions about the spaces they utilize affirms the importance of their opinions.

Managing Materials, Tools, and Resources

The selection of materials is essential to authentic artistic process. An organized and attractive arrangement of materials and tools permits young artists to access what they need and return excess for others' use. Waste is rarely an issue once students are familiar with classroom structure. Students care for materials and tools, an expectation of every good art program.

Each studio center prominently features directions and references, making information accessible to both readers and nonreaders. With these indirect teaching supports, students are able to work independently while their teacher interacts with classmates.

PRACTICE FOUR: ASSESSMENT

Choice-based art education utilizes multiple forms of assessment to support student and teacher growth.
(Douglas et al., 2002)

Assessment is ongoing, with students showing evidence of learning in their daily activities. Multiple assessments inform teaching, resulting in materials and instruction that are closely aligned with student needs. Observation is key to all assessment practices in the choice-based art class. Teachers create manageable methods for collecting data on student progress utilizing checklists, photo documentation, dialogues, and student writing.

It is important to include learners in discussions about assessment purposes. Teachers help students by introducing self-assessment tools such as journals, artist statements, sharing sessions, and electronic portfolios. Rubrics negotiated between students and teachers establish criteria for work throughout the year. Students use information gained in self-assessments to build confidence and measure their progress. Teachers use this information to redirect individualized and group instruction and to develop new curricula.

Collaboration

Assessment is often collaborative, merging student perspectives with teacher observations. Students working independently show what they know and can do. Effective assessment requires frequent feedback. The teacher circulates, witnessing artmaking in various stages of completion. Acknowledging all students, however briefly, during class encourages them to "engage and persist" (Hetland et al., 2007, pp. 42–47) through the ups and downs of their work. Some conversations are long, others short and specific. Redirecting and affirming progress helps students to focus on attainable goals.

Collaborative assessment also includes student-to-student discussions about classmates' work. These conversations may be structured as pair shares, group shares, and class presentations. Learners consult each other and comment while working in natural and spontaneous ways.

Evaluation

Evaluations document student skills and understandings. Choice-based teachers recognize student potential for developing ideas, as divergent thinking is central to teaching for artistic behavior. In addition to skills, teachers acknowledge work habits, including persistence, risk taking, inquiry, and time management. These behaviors develop through continued practice with various artistic processes. All of these criteria have a place in evaluation and reporting progress to families.

Exhibition

Students select artwork to exhibit, and their choices reflect self-evaluation of their recent work. Empowering students to organize and direct art shows extends their knowledge to the fields of aesthetics and criticism. As they determine which pieces to exhibit and how to arrange the exhibition, students develop skills necessary for growth in the visual arts.

PUTTING THE FOUR PRACTICES IN CONTEXT

Orchestrating personal, pedagogical, classroom, and assessment practices into a well-defined art program requires perseverance and dedication. To the untrained eye, teaching for artistic behavior may appear to be simple and easy to manage. Successful choice-based teachers invest significant time preparing the learning environment while planning instruction and assessment. The outcome of this hard work is a smoothly functioning art studio for independent work. Those familiar with this teaching concept appreciate the infrastructure as a carefully designed equilibrium, organic in nature yet solid in practice.

PROVIDING THE RATIONALE FOR CHOICE-BASED ART EDUCATION

Inform your school community about your desire to teach using the choice-based practice. This concept may be new to your administrators, your school colleagues, and parents; be proactive in offering information right from the beginning. Reassure administrators that the philosophy of teaching for artistic behavior aligns with both state and national visual art standards (see Appendix A). Each district's visual art curriculum is incorporated into the resources and demonstrations throughout the school year. Connect choice-based art education with other areas of the school curriculum that reflect similar practices. For example, language arts teachers look to the habits of writers to teach children how to write (Ray, 2002) and also encourage children to pursue personal topics in their writing (Calkins, 1994). Use all of this information to draft a plan for making the transition to student-centered learning. A succinct presentation of the benefits of a choice-based art program, such as those highlighted in Sidebar 1.1 will go a long way toward creating administrative support.

Communicate often with your school community through newsletters and Web logs which explain and celebrate learner-directed accomplishments. Local newspapers are happy to feature art room happenings, and teaching for artistic behavior offers a new slant on education. Make brief presentations at parent council or school board meetings, where vivid examples of student work illustrate good outcomes. Our students are by far our best advocates. The enthusiasm and joy they exhibit about their artwork will be conveyed to parents and school colleagues alike.

Sidebar 1.1. Ten Benefits of a Choice-Based Art Program in Elementary and Middle Schools

- Visual arts standards are covered in instruction.
- Teaching and learning addresses studio practice, art history, concepts, and aesthetics.
- Assessment supports both student and teacher growth.
- Higher order thinking skills are the norm for independent work.
- Differentiation addresses diverse learners' needs.
- High engagement results in students on-task, fewer discipline issues and success for at-risk learners.
- Technology is embedded in artmaking, research, and assessment practices.
- Integration and extension of classroom curricula is supported for interested students.
- Time, space, and resources—often scarce—are utilized efficiently in the art studio learning environment.
- A safe environment sustains deep learning for all.

Plate P.1.
Student artists from choice-based classes across the United States exhibit their work in the Arnheim Gallery in Boston.

Plate 1.1.
Students use visual references for their own purposes. Here a first grader distills the essence of a tiger from a book about animals.

Plate 2.1.
Each studio center provides organized materials, directions, and visual references.

Plate 2.2. This studio construction center provides easy access to a variety of resources. Menus posted on the cabinet reinforce simple directions and vocabulary.

Plate 2.3. Smaller studio centers, such as this soft sculpture center, can be contained in boxes and taken out as needed.

Plate 3.1. The Five-Minute Museum sparks new ideas and exposes students to the work of adult artists.

Plate 3.2. A student weaves independently, expanding on skills she learned earlier in the year.

Plate 4.1. A kindergarten boy shares his discoveries at the painting studio center with a friend.

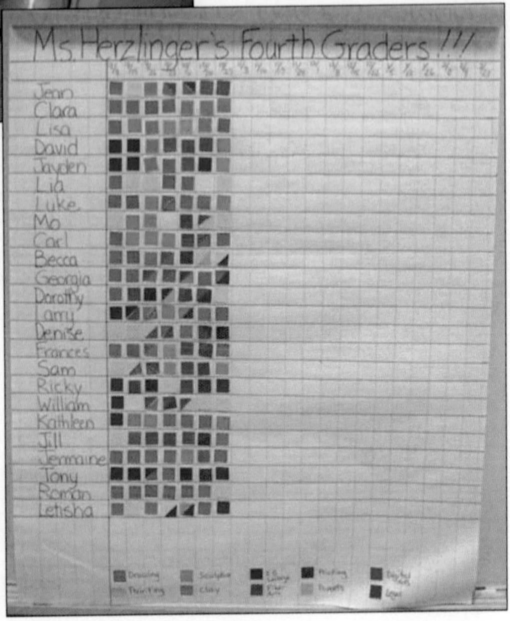

Plate 4.2. Students chart their progress using color coding to represent various studio centers.

Plate 5.1. Powerful ideas motivate students to make plans outside of art class.

Plate 6.1. Internet displays provide excellent opportunities for students to share their work inside and outside of school.

Plate 6.2. Artist statements accompany exhibited artwork, bringing the voice of the students to a community art show.

Plate 8.1.
Some painters
count sketching
as one of
their artistic
behaviors;
others work
spontaneously.

Plate 9.1.
"This is someone doing
gymnastics over the bar.
I did this when we were
learning about joints in
art class. When Sam was
posing, it reminded me
of gymnastics. I pasted
shapes around the
person to fill the paper."
Mikaela, Grade 3

Plate 9.2.
Fifth graders
collaborate to solve
structural challenges in
their sculpture.

Plate 9.3. "The idea for Cork Divas popped into my head when I saw corks and puff balls next to each other. In the scene, the cork friends are dancing and singing, having a good time. They are totally imaginary. I developed the idea as I went along. I just kept thinking about how cool it would be in the end." Jaime, Grade 3

Plate 10.1. Stamping is a familiar technique for most students and offers a bridge into printmaking practices.

Plate 10.2. A small monoprint studio center holds everything students need, while confining the mess to one small area.

Plate 10.3.
A printmaker
contemplates
her next moves
on a series of
silkscreen prints.

Plate 10.4.
Students take responsibility
for setting up their work area,
labeling, and putting their clay
artwork on shelves to dry.

Plate 11.1.
This studio center offers
multiple possibilities for
puppet creation and drama.

CHAPTER 2

The Learning Environment

The well-designed center is a three-dimensional lesson plan.
(Crowe, 2002a)

In choice-based art classrooms, teachers become architects, thinking about issues of space, traffic flow, proximity to resources, and arrangement of supplies and lighting. Designing a cluster of studio centers to meet the diverse needs of artists is a complex task. With careful planning, the art classroom can be arranged to display an enormous number of resources and materials that facilitate both group and independent work. A consistent layout allows students to work with the comfort of familiarity. Choice-based teachers find themselves refining studio centers each year to improve teaching and learning effectiveness.

ANATOMY OF A STUDIO CENTER

John Crowe's "three-dimensional lesson" plan is a good metaphor for studio centers, which serve as the hub for materials and tools and also as indirect teaching tools. Studio centers are designed to accommodate diverse learning styles and artistic behaviors. Organized studio centers contain directions, materials, tools, and resources, as seen in Plate 2.1, allowing learners to pursue work while their teacher interacts with other students. When structuring for independent work, remember that both first-time and frequent users need ready access to resources at each studio center.

Menus

Each center contains one or more menus highlighting site-specific information. Menus are simplified lists of directions or sequenced steps and vocabulary. Drawings or photographs can accompany menu items for nonreaders. Small laminated menus can be tucked into pockets attached to the larger menus. Children can carry these with them as they get ready to work. Plate 2.2 exhibits menus for a construction center.

Materials and Tools

Organized arrangement of materials and tools is key to creating an effective center. Provide color-coded containers that are easy to access, carry, and find at cleanup time. Sorted materials are visually inspiring: markers with caps up in cups are more inviting than a box with markers thrown into it. Topal and Gandini (1999) recommend clear plastic containers. Contents are appealing and easy to distinguish as students select their materials. Some teachers keep a few general tools such as scissors, tape, and glue in each center, while others have a central location for these items. Logical arrangement of supplies permits efficient access and return of art materials.

Resources

Large and small centers contain additional resources. Vocabulary words are posted along with visual examples. Photographs and reproductions of artwork from varied eras and cultures are displayed on bulletin boards or in folders when space is lacking. Easy-to-access files of reference materials and reproductions are also useful. Art books, exemplary picture books, and nonfiction resources can be placed in each center. Student work can also be displayed in centers along with photos of art being made. When possible, use the walls adjacent to the centers for visuals. Portable bulletin boards also work well for this purpose. Small folded cards containing vital information can be placed in working areas that lack wall space.

Furniture

Art teachers are the best scroungers! They patrol their schools, homes, and yard sales, seeking the bookcase, table, or rack that will define a space, hold information, or provide yet another workspace in their classroom studios. You can often find discarded items in school hallways just prior to the start of the school year as classroom teachers set up their rooms and older furniture is exchanged for newer pieces. Analyze the contents of your classroom and determine what you will need. Is there sufficient storage in each area? A lot of shelving makes supplies readily available and can be used for storing student work. Do you have enough tables to provide working spaces for five or more centers? Remember that students can also work on the floor and many prefer that option. Offer workspaces with and without chairs to suit student needs. Dividers create smaller spaces within the large space of the room. If you feel that your furnishings are not sufficient, start with what you have and plan to add as opportunities arise.

ROOM ARRANGEMENT

Spend time observing and responding to traffic and work patterns in the art room. Children are not confined to one seat as in some classrooms. Students will move about the room gathering materials, tools, and references. Some centers will be more popular and need more space. Tables may be set aside as overflow areas, allowing for an ebb and flow of use, which varies from class to class. See Sidebar 2.1 for a list of things to consider when arranging your art room.

Placement of Centers

Arrangement of centers within the classroom will depend upon the structure of your room. The facilities, storage, carpeting, sink, white board, and windows all factor in as you decide where to place each center. It makes sense to keep painting close to the water source. The sculpture center requires additional storage for materials and student work. The clay center needs space for work to dry safely before firing. Students at the drawing center appreciate natural light when possible. Each classroom presents unique challenges, which teachers resolve in many ways. Some divide their classrooms into wet and dry areas for simplification. Look around your room and decide what will work best for you and your students.

Sidebar 2.1. Room Arrangement Considerations

1. What are the most common traffic patterns?
2. Should you have a wet side and dry side of the art room?
3. Can you locate clean centers such as computers, drawing, and book references away from messier ones?
4. Will you have a central location for tools?
5. Where will unfinished two- and three-dimensional work be stored?
6. Where is the drying area for wet artworks?
7. If you have portfolios or class boxes, where will they be stored and how will students access them?
8. Are all visible materials available for student use? If not, how will this be made evident without reminders from you?
9. Are centers and materials color-coded?
10. Will you have a quiet area?
11. Can you provide a place for everyone to sit at the beginning and end of each class?

Meeting Area/Demo Area

Choice-based art classes start with a demonstration. Establish a central area where all students can see you. In smaller classrooms, students are seated together at centers. Larger classrooms may provide space adjacent to the whiteboard for this purpose, with students seated on the floor. Students return to the designated meeting area at the end of class to share and reflect. Take time to design an attractive teaching space that will support both of these whole-class gatherings.

Prep Area

If you have a large room, you can set aside a teacher-only corner where you store supplies and equipment to be used throughout the year. In some schools classroom teachers frequent the art room to get supplies and to cut paper. Providing other staff members with a small place to work goes a long way toward building collegiality.

CHALLENGING LEARNING ENVIRONMENTS

In some schools, space for the art program is compromised. Imperfect teaching and learning situations are served well by choice-based art education because of its flexibility. It may actually be easier to manage a problem room using studio centers.

Substandard Spaces

If you teach in a room lacking running water and windows, or a space shared with other classes, or a hallway, you are working in a substandard space. Nonetheless, you are going to make the best of it for your students and yourself. In a room without a sink, strict limits are placed on the number of painters at any one time, with more options available for those using dry media. In a small room, centers can be tiny and fit into plastic containers. Carefully selected materials and folders of laminated information are placed in the box for easy referral. Students get their materials from the container and bring them to work areas. In a classroom with many windows, there may be insufficient bulletin board space. Some teachers hang menus, reproductions, and vocabulary words from the ceiling. One teacher actually mounted laminated information flat on the ceiling for children to look up and see! Tables can have menus and information attached directly to the work surface. A small room requires exquisite organization, but that is a plus in any art room.

Sharing a room with another art teacher or specialist is an exercise in tact and cooperation, no matter what sort of program you teach. If materials are going to be used by two art teachers and only one is choice-based, centers may have to come out of storage while teaching for artistic behavior. After-school programs frequently share art rooms. One teacher with this situation placed her studio centers next to cabinets. Students in her last class knew how to pack everything into the closed cabinets. Her morning students unpacked and set up the centers once again. Whatever your teaching situation, there is a way to adapt your program for a good fit.

Art on a Cart

Many art teachers work without a designated teaching space. They may be given a small closet to store materials, sometimes without enough room even for a desk. If these are your circumstances, you are to be admired for your willingness to consider adapting your program. The following tips will help make this transition manageable even under difficult conditions.

Consider each center to be contained in one or two boxes. Copy paper boxes are excellent for most centers as they are sturdy and come with a strong lid. Wet materials, such as paint and clay need plastic containers with tight-fitting lids. Attach menus and visual resources onto the sides of the box as a permanent reference for students. Think carefully about the contents and arrange them so that students can take materials out and return them with little effort, as in Plate 2.3. Keep paper separate from other materials so it stays clean and crisp.

Your cart is your lifeline! Arrange it so that each center sits on one shelf, with extras tucked into leftover space. Pockets and containers are attached to the sides of the cart for extra storage. As you enter each classroom, designated students quickly take the boxes to prearranged tables and lay out the materials. Consistency is key, so little time is wasted setting up and breaking down the mobile centers. Assure each teacher that the classroom will be restored to order, as students will be highly motivated to maintain these centers for their artmaking.

Remember that working from a cart requires far more physical stamina than working in a classroom. Because you will need to conserve your energy, a word about stress management is necessary in this situation. Limit choices to three or four centers at a time. Students will have ample choices from the media you have selected for them. Change the offerings every 2 or 3 months, keeping the most popular studio centers available throughout the year. Maintain a balance between teaching for artistic behavior and managing your own health and sanity while working under less-than-ideal conditions.

High Student Mobility

Teaching for artistic behavior programs empower learners who enter at any point during the school year. New students, including English language learners, observe multiple activities and are able to get right to work. In schools with high levels of student mobility, peer coaching becomes a necessity. Experienced students enjoy helping their new classmates.

Year-Round Schools

In districts with schools in session throughout the year, students and teachers are continually in flux. The consistency of studio centers enables students to anticipate their art activities despite long periods away from the art room. Colorado teacher Dale Zalmstra sees multiple grade levels every day for a week, and then not again for several weeks' time. She builds momentum, adding concepts and materials as the week progresses. Because students pace themselves, they can choose to continue on their work when art class resumes, or move to something new. This alleviates some of the problems that teacher-directed art programs may encounter in year-round school schedules.

BEYOND THE CLASSROOM

Choice-based art education has tremendous potential in learning environments outside the school day. In an out-of-school-time program for adolescents designed by students at Massachusetts College of Art and Design, authentic artmaking provides an appealing opportunity for students. The challenge for preservice teachers here is to create and administer an engaging art program despite unique obstacles. Complications arise with fluctuating attendance and the emotional and physical needs of students who have been in school all day. Community art practices address these issues and focus on student artists who may be disenfranchised by the system. This program encourages students to produce art that comes out of the wellspring of the community and out of their own lives and interests. This makes a good fit with choice-based teaching and learning. John Giordano (personal communication, March 14, 2007), who oversees the program comments:

> Because one of the primary goals of youth development is to help students make better life decisions, the curriculum should support making choices in a thoughtful way. In a nutshell, we give structure, hear the

kids, and respond in our offerings. It is a successful learning experience for the middle school students and the MassArt students.

Summer camps are also excellent sites for choice-based art education. At one camp all art materials are available as soon as they are introduced to the children. Several large tables are open for all types of work during scheduled classes and unscheduled time. Children access their tools and materials from one central location in the art room. Large menus are visible across the room and support independent learning in this informal setting.

THE LEARNING ENVIRONMENT IS A WORK IN PROGRESS

A dynamic learning environment requires close observation and continual adjustments. Your initial arrangements will evolve based on the needs of your particular student body. Talk with your students and get their input. Since they are the ones using the centers, they have the best ideas about how the centers function. Be sure to include your students in the ongoing development of the learning environment.

CHAPTER 3

How to Structure the Class

The job of the artist is to have an art idea and find the best material to express it or
to find a material that leads to an idea.
(P. Joseph, personal communication, October 27, 2003)

A good friend once compared a choice-based classroom to the large and busy South Station in Boston. People are constantly in motion, people are getting information from various sources, people are coming from a variety of places and heading in a great many directions. When one looks across the room it may seem a bit confusing, but each rail commuter has a destination and knows where to get the required information and ticket (C. Wood, personal communication, September 14, 2002). Likewise, children in our classrooms are headed in many directions; but without effective classroom management, chaos would reign.

A NEW PERSPECTIVE ON TEACHING AND LEARNING

Teaching for artistic behavior differs from more traditional teaching methodology. In order for students to direct their learning, the teacher must limit whole-group instruction to essential information (Runco, 2007) and then step back. Explicit lesson plans that define all the choices prevent students from being original. In choice-based practice some students will respond to the demo during studio time and others will not. Show respect for the choices students make and offer support as needed. During studio time the instructor circulates and may do any of several things:

- Offer small-group and individual assistance
- Facilitate solutions
- Provide additional instruction and reinforcement for those ready for more information.
- Highlight an interesting piece of student work
- Make connections between their work and adult artists' work:

"I see that you are making a collage that includes people. Did you know that another artist named Romare Beardon often included people in his collages too? Here are some reproductions of his work."

"I notice that you have designed a box to hold your papers and pencils. Some adults do the same kind of work for their job. They are called industrial designers."

As time allows, sit with students and work alongside them while conversing about struggles and happy discoveries. Modeling can be the most effective teaching!

For students new to this pedagogy, the learning environment will look different from the last time they were in art class. The teacher should explain: "After watching you work these past years, I have decided that we need a different kind of art program. We will have studio centers that address all of your interests and growth as artists. As the year progresses, we will be talking much more about the many choice opportunities you will experience in art class." Students returning to a choice-based art program will proceed directly to drawing, painting, sculpture, and other centers after the introductory demo. Everyone is excited to get started making art!

MODES OF INSTRUCTION

Classes are structured into segments: demonstration, studio, cleanup, and sharing and reflection (see Appendix B). Some students have problems transitioning into art class. Size up the class as children enter the art room. Greet them at the door or even in the hallway outside your room if space allows. Make eye contact with each child and greet those who may need extra attention. Depending upon your room setup, students can be seated at tables or in a circle on the floor. Whatever your beginning routine is, keep it consistent. When children know what to expect, they will respond more quickly to the information you have planned for them.

Whole-Group Instruction: The Five-Minute Demo

What is the very *least* students need to know in order to begin their art-making? They need to know basic information about new materials or techniques and how to get started. It is a challenge to show this in just 5 minutes. Students need significant time to do their artwork so a brief demonstration, known as the *demo,* is essential. This requires careful planning to condense information to a bare minimum, as shown by the examples in Sidebars 3.1

Sidebar 3.1. Examples of Choice-Based Demonstrations

Clay. For children who have never experienced natural clay, discussion begins while small pieces of clay are passed around for students to feel.

"What do you think clay is made of?"
"Where do you think it comes from?"

Techniques can then be shown: rolling clay into worms or a ball, making a pinch pot, forming an animal. A quick word about scoring attachments will be reinforced while students are working. The same applies to wedging the clay should students want to restart their ideas.

Fibers. To help students with embroidery, the main idea is this: "If you can draw it, you can stitch it!" Visuals reinforce steps for threading a needle and tying a knot. A simple sketch on scrap paper is duplicated with chalk on dark colored burlap. The running stitch and backstitch are briefly demonstrated. Resources are posted in the fiber arts center where the teacher remains on the first day.

Sidebar 3.2. The Five-Minute Museum

One morning four large reproductions are shown to the entire class: a non-objective painting, a still life, a portrait, and a landscape. Children view and discuss these very briefly. This is the *why* of painting now that they have played around with the *how*. These occasional demos start with some reproductions and quick sound bites about the artists' lives. Then students move to centers to begin their artwork.

Images in the Five-Minute Museum are related by theme or medium (see Plate 3.1). The purpose is to briefly expose students to the work of adult artists. The class that does a lot of construction benefits from seeing the work by Calder, Segal, or Sarah Sze. Interested students continue to view and discuss images after their classmates have moved to studio centers. Reproductions influence students' directions; keeping them on display enables further examination during class time.

and 3.2. Teacher decisions about demo content originate in district curriculum, national and local standards, art history, and also in emergent student needs and interests. All students attend these demonstrations, which are highly organized, concise expositions of information. Supporting resources are permanently available in studio centers.

Students in all classrooms make choices about what to remember, what to forget, and the level of involvement to bring to the work. Children in learner-centered classrooms are encouraged to make their own connections and "form their own purposes" (Eisner, 2002, p. 51). Core information is available not only in the demos, but in menus, exemplars, technology, and books. Students access what they need to do their work.

Small-Group, Individual, and Peer Instruction: Studio Time

Many students know ahead exactly what they are going to do and will quickly go to a specific center as soon as the demo is over. Others may pause as they try to decide where to begin. During this transition from demo to studio centers, the teacher assists students making choices about work and materials. In Plate 3.2, a child has decided to revisit weaving, a process she learned earlier in the school year.

Learners provide much of the instruction at studio centers. Those who work repeatedly in a particular direction serve as coaches and mentors, reinforcing further learning in the process. The teacher has a good sense of which children have experience and can refer newcomers directly to them. Many children prefer to learn from a classmate than from a grown-up. Peer coaches, who might be among the least capable children in the academic realm, get validation from helping their classmates. Some learners form collaborative groups and pool information. With so many options available, students demonstrate expertise at various times in various domains. This results in many opportunities for students to mentor and to be mentored.

Learners work at their own pace, determining when they are finished. If students abandon uncompleted work, as artists sometimes do, a short consult with the teacher establishes a new path. Everyone has a job and everyone is doing his or her job. There is no such thing as the *do-nothing center*! Students who show that they need more structure will get it.

Student Responsibilities: Cleanup

Establish clear and simple routines for cleanup with real consequences for a job poorly done. Teachers set up and stock centers but do not have time to clean them daily. Children are responsible for maintaining the studios where they work and leaving them tidy and organized for the next group. By their actions, children show what they need and can manage. A poorly cleaned center may indicate any of the following:

- Insufficient time for cleanup
- Poor organization at the center
- Unfamiliarity with expectations and routines
- Unwillingness to take responsibility

Near cleanup time, the teacher calls attention to the clock and offers strategies for preparing to leave the art room. Children review their work and decide to bring it to a conclusion or save it for the next class. Artwork is brought to a central location to go home or remain in the work-in-progress box. Housekeeping should happen in less than 3 minutes. Inform students that you will be timing their cleanup to see how many minutes they will need in future weeks. If a new studio center has just been introduced, gather the class and point out the specifics of cleanup. After everything has been put away properly, announce that the class has earned the grand opening of another studio center, or additional materials if all studio centers are already open. The consequence of a poor cleanup is loss of the particular studio center at the next class. When students indicate that they are ready to handle responsibility, they earn back the lost center. Once the room is back in order, children retrieve their artwork to share with classmates.

Student Understandings: Reflection

Have a set routine for the conclusion of art class to give children a sense of closure. There are a number of ways to share work at the end of class. This is particularly important when teaching for artistic behavior because of the many different activities in each class. As with the demo, time is extremely limited and must be preserved for this purpose.

Sharing. As soon as the room looks ready, children in primary grades claim their pieces and begin their pair share. "Find a friend. Ask, 'What did you do today?'" This is the beginning of looking at and talking about art. Some students will ask ahead to share with the whole class. The artist waits for eye contact from everybody and speaks clearly. The group is invited to comment or ask a question of the artist. Various interchanges reveal understanding at many levels:

"I really like it."
"How did you mix that color?"
"What is it?"
"That reminds me of the playground."

If time does not allow for individual sharing, groups of students who worked at the same center can hold their work up for all to see. Sharing, comments, and questions become increasingly sophisticated and thoughtful with practice.

Questioning for Understanding. Sometimes instead of looking at student work, toss out some questions to the class:

"Who made an amazing discovery today?"

"Who had a struggle today? Did you overcome your problem? If not, can anyone suggest a strategy for the artist?" *Strategy* refers to useful tactics that artists find not only from their teacher but also from peers and trial and error.

"Who learned something new from a classmate?" This elicits responses about collaboration, a form of learning that is highly effective.

Journals. Students in intermediate grades maintain journals in which they record their efforts at the end of class. When class time is short, small journals hold quick notes and diagrams of the day's work. Time for writing in journals can be expanded on occasion for deeper insights and goal setting. As the year progresses, students refer back to their journals to reflect on their directions in art class.

Classroom teachers who come early to pick up their groups enjoy the sharing and reflection as much as their students. Review as children line up. Ask a question from the lesson demonstration, such as "What is one true fact about color mixing?" One hand goes up and the student speaks, earning a place in line. Then lots of hands go up and more students join the line after telling a true fact. Finding a special way to conclude art classes will make this transition go smoothly for all.

RULES FOR SUCCESS

Setting Parameters

A review of classroom rules reminds students that they are responsible for their actions. Rules should be worded so that the language is clear to all students. In developing parameters for classroom behavior, balance your school's core values with curriculum needs and personal beliefs. If you work with a wide range of ages, you may establish developmentally appropriate rules for different age groups. Invite your older students to help write the rules and then be sure to maintain consistency.

Behave Like an Artist

Younger children respond well to these three simple rules:

Take care of people.
Take care of stuff.
Behave like an artist.

"Behave like an artist?" Unless children have spent a lot of time in art studios, they are not going to know what it means to behave like an artist. What exactly is it that artists do, and how can teachers encourage the same behaviors in their students? Explain to students that playing and experimenting with art materials are artistic behaviors. Talking about art ideas with classmates is also an artistic behavior, along with making sketches first or not making sketches first. Each student develops a unique combination of behaviors that form the foundation for his or her own creative process. Many of these artistic behaviors influence work in other disciplines, so "behave like an artist" is a very good rule to enforce!

TAKING CARE OF BUSINESS

You will find that much of your time during the first weeks of school is taken up with nonteaching obligations. Schedule adjustments, class lists, Individual Educational Plans, unpacking supplies, staff meetings all encroach on your available time. Try to find a few quiet moments to reflect. Make a list of the artworks you have seen or interesting behaviors witnessed during the

---

Sidebar 3.3. Curriculum Mapping

Based on the work of Heidi Hayes Jacobs (2004), curriculum mapping is a good way to track the diversity of ideas, 5-minute demos, and learning in a choice-based art room. Curricular maps are created by documenting what really happens. They are typically calendar based, but can be designed around curricular themes and can help art teachers connect with the work of regular classrooms. Maps can be tailored to meet the needs of the teacher and the school. Mapping provides information for administrators, parents, and the community to know what is being taught in the art program.

Setting up a curriculum map is easy and requires very little time to maintain. Each map should contain essential ideas, content taught, skills, and any assessments used to gauge a child's progress. Weekly or biweekly, the teacher notes exactly what was taught. This continues throughout the year. At the end of the year a month-by-month document reflects what actually happened in the art room. Using this information, revise areas of difficulty and retool your plan for the coming year. Over time, this gives you and your administrators a clear picture of the breadth and depth of your curriculum, both horizontally (month-to-month) and vertically (elementary-to-high school). In choice-based teaching and learning, curriculum mapping provides organization and an assessment record of the year.

— Clark Fralick (2007)

course of the week. Curriculum mapping is a method to reflect on the directions of your classes, as described in Sidebar 3.3.

Think about what you have you learned about your students during their first week of school. Think also about how you can present your choice-based art program to parents at a curriculum night or PTO meeting. Sidebar 3.4 offers suggestions for ways to build support. Your observations and comments will influence how adults view learner-directed pedagogy in the art program.

Sidebar 3.4. Back-to-School Night

Most schools schedule a curriculum night early in the year to communicate about teaching and learning goals. Let your principal know that you would like to participate so parents can learn more about teaching for artistic behavior. Choice-based art teacher Bonnie Muir (2004) writes enthusiastically about her first Back-to-School Night:

> Tell parents how excited you are about teaching children and that you value their ideas and their work. Give parents a taste of what their child will be experiencing in the art program and you will reach your audience. I mention that our art curriculum is aligned with the state frameworks. I talk about my philosophy of teaching and I speak about the child as artist. My students are expected to take care of the art room and materials to learn responsibility. I let parents know that I value process as well as product, and that children's art does not need to look like adult work. Understanding this shows respect for students' ideas and values. I talk about the centers offered in my room and what materials children will be working with. Copies of my wish list (magazines, glue sticks, paper tubes, and so on) are available, and include my request for parent volunteers. At the bottom of this letter I include the best way to reach me. Parents are such a good group of people to have on your side!

Encourage parents to visit the art room on Back-to-School Night. What will they see if they step into your classroom? Centers are set up with materials, tools, and resources, a good way to introduce teaching for artistic behavior. Some teachers invite parents to sit down and make art; others have a slide show playing in the background, showing images of students at work. An exhibit of artwork by all students would be cumbersome in this venue; however, a few representative pieces can be placed on display.

CHAPTER 4

Assessing Progress

The appearance of understandings is not a sufficient indicator
of actual understanding.
(Beghetto & Plucker, 2006, p. 323)

What does learning look like in the choice-based art class? Children are engaged in art experiences by themselves or in collaborative groups. Their talk is centered on their work. Exclamations ring out as a breakthrough is made. Important questions about strategies, technique, or the order of colors in the rainbow can be heard above the hum of activity. The teacher moves around the room, making observations, taking notes, mentally planning for the weeks ahead while assisting in knot tying and color mixing. Tomlinson (1999) states that instruction and assessment go hand in hand; this is highly evident when teaching for artistic behavior. Effective instruction requires teachers to be aware of what is and is not working for students. Assessments inform teachers about student understandings, needs, and artistic behaviors. State standards guide teachers in planning instruction and assessment to make certain that students receive a comprehensive education.

HIGH EXPECTATIONS

Nan Hathaway once had to defend her choice-based program to a visitor who asked, "Can the kids just do anything they want? And can they do it all the time?" Key to this question is the word *just,* because to uninformed adults it may seem that the work is trivial and nondirected. When responding to the "do anything they want" question, stress that, because students have chosen their work, there are higher expectations of them. Children work toward greater mastery because they are highly invested in pursuing their ideas. Consider the complexity of what students, even kindergarteners, are asked to do:

- Find an idea
- Select materials to express the idea
- Arrange those materials plus tools in a workspace
- Pace themselves
- Create the image or structure
- Overcome obstacles
- Return materials and tools to their proper location
- Discuss artwork and reflect on progress

FORMATIVE ASSESSMENTS

Student achievement varies according to experience. Formative assessments identify student skills and understandings at individual developmental stages (Saphier & Gower, 1997) for the purpose of setting goals and planning curriculum. Artwork alone cannot provide sufficient information for assessment. Individual artworks may show a student's ideas and technical ability, but there is much more about thinking and learning that will become evident when the teacher listens to students talking about their work. Children mentor one another as they work, giving tips and information. Those new to centers ask questions, which are thoughtfully answered. Discussions about work in progress are more prevalent than one might expect, as in the case of the two boys pictured in Plate 4.1.

Affirmation of students' efforts is ongoing throughout each class. Teachers watch for a discovery and then objectively state an observation: "I notice that Sarah has found a strategy to show space in her painting by making the trees in the background smaller than the girl in the foreground." Students often take on this role as well, coaching and cheering their classmates for their large and small accomplishments. This kind of peer support is well received and encourages greater risk taking in future classes.

Much can be learned about a student's developing artistic behavior by careful observation. Select a student, someone about whom you know little. Make a point to observe this child for several minutes at the beginning, middle, and end of class. How does the student set up materials and begin to work? Is the same piece pursued throughout class, or are there several different efforts? Does this learner work alone or collaborate with classmates? How is the transition to cleanup time managed? It is a fascinating study to see how every child grows as an artist.

Conferences and Conversations

> *My Uncle Jason taught me how to make dragons a long time ago. I started to get*
> *better and better as I got older. I decided to draw a dragon on the chalkboard, and*
> *then start a bigger painting. It took me about 3 art classes to do; it was hard to de-*
> *cide the colors. I had to mix a lot of the colors and add a lot of details and designs.*
> *I had to think about how I was going to pose him. I changed my mind a whole lot.*
> —Ashley, Grade 3

Elements of students' creative process are not always evident in the finished work (Hetland et al., 2007). Conversations such as Ashley's provide
insight into her thinking and artistic behaviors. As time allows, teachers talk
with students formally and informally. Discussions are brief so that they do
not impact studio time. Conferences may be motivated by a connection the
teacher would like to suggest, an observation that may influence future work,
or observed behaviors for the student to expand or cease. According to Tomlinson (2001):

> A teacher who understands the need for teaching and learning to be a good
> match for students looks for every opportunity to know her students better.
> She sees conversations with individuals, classroom discussions, student work,
> observation, and formal assessment as a way to gather just a little more insight
> about what works for each learner. What she learns becomes a catalyst for craft-
> ing instruction in ways that help each student make the most of his potential
> and talents. (p. 4)

In studio centers students constantly demonstrate what they know and can
do on their own. Choice-based teachers can differentiate for individual artistic behaviors and preferences readily because they know their students well.
No one is invisible in art class.

Documenting Evidence of Learning

Keep assessment records of student learning; these come in handy when
sharing information with other adults and when filling out progress reports.
School districts may offer assessment instruments and require grading; more
often, art teachers develop their own assessments to match instruction. Clyde
Gaw teaches students to maintain electronic portfolios of their work in art
class (see Sidebar 4.1).

Individual teachers have developed strategies to keep organized records.
For example, Carolyn Kinniery marks studio centers visited by every student
during the art class in her record book. A simple code, such as *P* for painting
and *Cl* for clay indicates the student's direction. On separate charts with cen-

---

Sidebar 4.1. Electronic Portfolios in the Choice Art Room

Electronic portfolios enhance student's artistic experience in the choice-based art program and there are several reasons teachers may want to integrate them into their curriculum. From an assessment and accountability standpoint, electronic portfolios allow teachers easy access to student work. Students creating electronic portfolios engage in metacognitive thinking and employ new linguistic, digital, and visual literacy skills. Discovery learning takes place as students work with electronic media, observe new perspectives and synthesize new learning and skills while documenting their work on the computer.

Working portfolios are collections of files that might contain images, word documents, movies, or audio of students engaged in artistic experiences. Presentation portfolios can be developed for specific situations or events by editing and polishing the contents of the working portfolio. When possible, use a digital camera to capture images of art and students in the act of artistic experience. These images will provide your students with rich source material from which to write and think reflectively. Think carefully about what you want students to accomplish in a writing task. The sky is the limit!

After you have had a little practice, begin teaching one student at a time about electronic portfolios. Select students to train others. Soon you will have your program up and running. The more you use electronic media, the more skillful you and your students will become. Word documents, audio, movies and other files can be hyperlinked so your portfolios are multidimensional. Electronic portfolios take time and effort; however, the dividends of intellectual and creative growth will make this endeavor extremely satisfying. Before you know it, *presto!* Just remember to start small and grow big.

—Clyde Gaw (2007)

---

ters written across the top, she adds students' names as they visit the center and quick details about their work.

Bonnie Muir's gridded charts list names of students in the first column, with one page for each class. All the class charts are laminated and bound together with rings, to facilitate flipping pages to the current class. Students mark colors next to their names, each color representing a particular center (see Plate 4.2 for a similar system). At a glance, students and teacher see which centers are being used; also, comparisons are easily made among classes. Students maintain these charts and check their own progress frequently.

Surveys

Teachers use action research to study student opinions. When children realize that they can influence curricular decisions, they are likely to be very honest. Write a question on a large sheet of paper and give students stickers to indicate their preference. For example, the question Were you satisfied with the location of your artwork in the school art show? can be answered with yes or no. Organize responses by grade level to identify developmental differences. Students can also conduct their own surveys and share the results at the end of class. Empower children to take ownership of their learning.

Journals and Student Reflections

Young artists are often so caught up in production that they need reminders to step back to reflect on all the good effort and thinking that go into their work. Journals enable learners to track their progress from week to week. Students draw or write what they accomplished during the class, dating each new page. This is a very brief notation or record. Later, using this data, students fill out self-reflections, indicating which centers they visit, significant work, and future goals.

The frequency and complexity of assigned self-reflections depends upon time available, age of students, and school requirements. Self-reflections provide students with opportunities to think deeply about their learning and artistic achievements. Writing about their *own* work is a rewarding experience for many students. Keep student writing focused with clearly worded questions or sentence starters to elicit the best results. Remember that certain students perform better orally so arrange to talk directly with these children. Here are some possible questions to ask students:

- Think about one of your artworks that you are proud of and describe it in three sentences.
- What is your favorite studio center? Why is it your favorite?
- Do you ever choose to work together with other students to collaborate on artwork? List three reasons why or why not.
- What was hard for you at the beginning of the year and is no longer hard?
- What would you like to get better at? How can that happen?

Collect data about the learning environment on the same questionnaires. When students critique studio centers, their responses result in improvements and set new directions for the curriculum.

Rubrics

In classroom settings, rubrics set parameters for specific class products, detailing criteria based on standards and indicating levels of performance.

Good rubrics outline clear expectations for students to demonstrate what they know and can do, with exemplars for each standard (Saphier & Gower, 1997). In choice-based classrooms, rubrics do not have to relate specifically to one artwork (see Sidebar 4.2). In fact, they can be designed to evaluate artistic behavior. Perseverance, resourcefulness, time management, and responsibility are criteria that could appear on an artistic behavior rubric. Children can help design the rubric and fill it out themselves.

Talking About Artwork

> *I named my altered book* MozArt *because if you look at my paintings in the book, they all seem unique, like Mozart is unique, too. A fun thing happened during my artmaking. My two friends were rating my pictures while I worked on them. If you look at the side of the pages, you will see what they think about my paintings.*
> —Veronica, Grade 5

While working, students receive both solicited and unsolicited comments from their classmates. For Veronica, a game of peer evaluations later became integrated into her artwork. Most students value their classmates' opinions and appreciate constructive criticism. Learning to filter out unhelpful remarks, however, is easier for some than others.

After cleanup, students convene for the sharing session. This is a time for the class to give full attention to their peers. An important aspect of this ses-

---

Sidebar 4.2. A Rubric for Excellence in Art Class

- Artists get ideas for their artwork from their personal experiences and interests, books, movies, other artists' work, and from art materials.
- Artwork shows good effort and planning.
- Artists include some of the elements of art such as line, color, pattern, texture, and shape, and use principles of art such as rhythm, contrast, and balance in their artwork.
- Artwork is complete. All areas and parts are carefully thought out and the artist is satisfied that the artwork is "done."
- All 3-D artwork is built to last. There are no loose pieces and no clay attachments that are not securely scored together.
- Artists show respect for materials and tools by cleaning up their workspace before moving to a new center and at the end of class.
- Artists show respect for classmates' artwork by not touching and by sharing positive comments.
- Artists are always productive in class with their own artwork or helping a classmate or teacher or researching ideas for future artworks.

—Burr School Fifth Grade Art Students (2004)

sion is self-reflection on the development of ideas and the artmaking process. Students revisit their steps and concentrate on the most significant details when they talk about their work. Some focus on technique, others on ideas or meaning. Still others may discuss an individual piece in the context of a larger series of artworks already completed.

PROGRESS REPORTS

Imagine evaluating over 600 students four times a year, filling out progress reports, and writing comments to parents about students' accomplishments! As impossible as this sounds, some elementary art teachers are expected to do this. This is why it is essential to keep clear, simple records to document each child's growth. Whether you have 100, 300, or 800 students, it is likely that you will be able to describe artistic behaviors that apply to many of your students. Nan Hathaway uses a reporting form that records areas of interest and observed growth (see Sidebar 4.3).

In large school districts, progress reports are standardized and there are few opportunities to give input on the wording of criteria. Those teaching in smaller school systems may be able to create their own progress reports. Look to the national standards when developing a progress report. It is important to convey to administrators and parents that teaching for artistic behavior meets all of the standards for visual arts (Appendix A).

Teachers often feel the need to comment about social behaviors on progress reports. This is rarely a concern in choice-based teaching since poor behavior often reflects frustration and lack of investment. Conduct is not among the content standards for visual arts and it does not belong as a standard in a progress report. If a child's behavior is less than satisfactory, address those issues directly with the parent. Families appreciate knowing details about their children's schoolwork. Positive anecdotes and observations can be shared through an e-mail, note, or phone call home, especially for those students whose school experiences are generally not positive. A few encouraging words can go a long way toward building trust and confidence.

TEACHER REFLECTION

Whether you take notes in your grade book, on your laptop, or reflect in a Web log or journal, these forms of documentation provide valuable testimony to the power of authentic learning. Assessment data is also useful as advocacy for choice-based teaching and learning. You may ask yourself, "How can I possibly do all this while I am maintaining centers?" It is possible and it

---

Sidebar 4.3. Progress Report

Areas of Interest: Which center does the student usually choose? What materials are preferred? What serves as inspiration for the student's work?

- Media
- Themes
- Specific projects

Observed Growth: In what ways does the student show growth/change in technique or approach?

- Planning/organization
- Innovations
- Risk taking
- Skill/technique development
- Meaning/expression
- Independence/collaboration
- Problem solving

—Nan Hathaway (2006b)

---

is important. Start with the simplest system with which you feel comfortable. Once that is in place, watch to see patterns of discovery learning emerge. Unlike classrooms where students primarily follow teacher directions, choice-based studio centers let learners show you what they really know and can do. This is authentic learning and assessment. Find quiet times during the school year when you can reflect on your classes and make decisions about the future.

CHAPTER 5

Ideas and Motivation

In time, as an artist's gestures become more assured, the chosen tools become almost an extension of the artist's own spirit. In time, exploration gives way to expression.
(Bayles & Orland, 1993, p. 59)

In choice-based classrooms, artwork does not take on the aspects of the "school art style" (Efland, 1976). Instead of assigning media, technique, and subject matter to produce a predictable product, the teacher focuses on core information. Decision making resides in student hands, and this shift in control may be disorienting for art teachers. Confidence, perseverance, risk taking, and innovation are true outcomes of authentic art teaching and learning. It takes tremendous trust to allow student work to be unexpected and unknown. There is a change in outcomes that takes place when control moves from teacher to student.

DISCOVERY LEARNING

When materials are first introduced, students have limited ideas of their possibilities. A playful and experimental approach results in sketches and collections of marks, useful for the maker but not necessarily for the viewer. Investment in exploratory play leads to rich artistic rewards. Students who have experimented with media expand their repertoire, making independent work more fruitful.

Children's play is intertwined with artmaking and deep learning. Experimentation results in innovation, and mistakes lead to surprising discoveries. Duckworth (1996, pp. 71–72) establishes that "wrong ideas" lead to deeper understanding when learners must reevaluate their concept. When students play and experiment, their teacher may feel that supplies are being used too quickly. Think hard about what actually constitutes waste. Practice and mistakes are honored when teaching for artistic behavior. These are necessary steps toward growth in artmaking. Demonstrations of warm-up and practice methods are helpful to students who fear making mistakes. Here are some examples:

1. Sketch on the chalkboard
2. Practice on scrap paper
3. Fold paper into four sections and sketch the same thing four times to
    warm up
4. Draw in a sketchbook
5. List plans
6. Paint out mistakes
7. Rework failed pieces
8. Chop up and reassemble pieces

As students work through their discoveries, their teacher comments on what is happening: "Notice how the paint runs around on that slippery paper—here is a more absorbent surface that you might want to try." "If you start with a pencil you might be able to end with markers once you are comfortable with what you have drawn." "Sometimes you can cut out the part of your drawing that pleases you and save it for later." "The paper trimmer can be used to cut off part of that and change the shape of your paper."

Andrew wrote a poem about his robot and how he envisions what is possible:

It is a robot
I drew the face.
I wish the nose could be a light bulb.
I wish the eyes could change colors.
I wish the mouth could speak every language.
I wish it could change form.
I wish he could make any food he wanted.
He could have anything he needed in his pouch.
I wish the bottom part that keeps him standing could hold a plate.
If you take him anywhere, you could take your food out and eat.

Like Andrew, many learners find a line of inquiry in the art classroom. When children choose ideas that fascinate them they are more likely to bring background knowledge to the work and to invest more care. Conversations unearth these interests and help students use them in artmaking. Andrew's robot idea took shape in his conversations with his teacher and friends. Student ideas may not find a home in other parts of school, so invite them into the studio.

Once students are comfortable with various materials and have begun expressing their own ideas and interests, you will begin to see—and should encourage—work that shows care. Some students may bring plans with them to class (see Plate 5.1). Ask students to generate lists of characteristics for quality work and share some exemplars. Quality does not always mean many weeks on one piece. Sketching with a purpose is quality work because the artist is improving drawing skills. Watercolor painting can be spontaneous and quick. The practice and play prevalent early in the year is for learning and finding direction. If you find that student work is not progressing, small changes in materials and resources will influence artists in new ways. Be patient; significant work will emerge in time.

MOTIVATION

Many factors, both internal and external, influence the quality of student artwork. Students who work from intrinsic motivation are likely to find more creative solutions (Amabile, 1996) and persevere as a result of that motivation (Runco, 2007). Teacher-assigned art projects may result in attractive solutions, but as an external motivation, explicit assignments are unlikely to bring out the best from all students. Here are some examples of intrinsic motivators that often lead to high-quality work in the choice-based art class:

- Artwork about the artist's interests
- Collaborative work with a good friend
- Desire for handmade playthings or objects
- Discovery of an intriguing material or tool

External factors that motivate some, but not all, students include:

- Special recognition from friends or family members
- Desire to please a teacher
- Artwork made as a special gift
- Deadlines for an exhibition

All students respond to positive acknowledgment of their efforts, and recognition from people they care about is important. Much of students' high-quality artwork goes home as gifts for family, though exhibition deadlines will likely motivate students to leave work at school for that purpose. Report card grades rarely motivate young students, as they do for some older students. High school art teacher Barb Andrews (2005) adds recognition through community service projects as an external motivation for her students. Completing a difficult task is a key factor in her students' investment in their achievement. Teaching for artistic behavior creates circumstances in which learners, not teachers, provide compelling motivation for quality work.

WHERE DO ART IDEAS COME FROM?

I rarely arrive at an idea by consciously sitting down at a desk and trying to figure out what I want to do. Once I start thinking about a project, though, it doesn't really leave my focus until I have come up with an idea.
—Lin, 2000 (p. 7)

Learning to develop strong ideas for artmaking takes much practice, often outside of the school day. Maya Lin speaks about her artistic behavior of centering on an idea. Young children also focus on ideas that are important to them. They arrive at art class preoccupied with personal passions and plans unknown to their teacher. These important ideas surfaced in the painting of a kindergartner named Jermaine:

This is a painting about skiing and walking home and having snowball fights and walking in the dark. All those fun things to do—it's fun but you have to stay close to home. If you are ski jumping, be sure to not go on the high jump unless you are older. I am going to ski when I turn 6.

In choice-based art classes, students ask each other how they get inspiration for their artwork, share ideas, and understand that images often come from something they've seen or experienced. Discoveries can flow directly from the media. Some children have a wealth of ideas and others will go to them for suggestions. Often this "idea person" pairs up with artists whose skills match their plan—kind of like the real world of business.

A bulletin board reads: Where Do Art Ideas Come From? Students from various grades list their own sources and where they think ideas of adult artists come from. The list collapses into basic groupings: nature, beliefs, family, traditions, culture, media, history, knowledge, other artists, and personal interests. Students consult this bulletin board if they need a start to their work.

Certain images repeatedly show up in art class. Often they have meaning for the artist and other times they are an easy entry for the student who lacks confidence. Rainbow drawings are one example. Instead of trying to discern meaning or the lack thereof, the teacher takes the image and shows how to push it further:

1. Search for Internet images of rainbows and rainbow art
2. Draw an uninspired rainbow and make it a challenge. Use words like *embellish, variation, reworking*

3. Dare students to paint, sculpt, print, and embroider rainbows, vary-
    ing size, repetitions, and patterns
4. Challenge students to come up with their own variations and post
    them on a bulletin board

Many student ideas originate in their subcultures of toys, games, and
favorite characters. These influences have a strong grasp on children; dis-
missing them as unsuitable subject matter for artmaking is likely to cause
problems. Sidebar 5.1 addresses the importance of establishing a climate of
respect for the culture that children embrace.

Integration with Classroom Curricula

Our study of the Wampanoag Native Americans is the inspiration for my artwork.
This is a model of a house called a wetu, *where the Wampanoags used to live. I*
made the wetu out of clay and I am proud of how I made the outside. You will see
figures representing a family of Wampanoags.
                                                           —Montana, Grade 3

When learning is truly integrated, curriculum will surface in places where
it did not originate. The learner synthesizes knowledge and applies it to new
situations. Montana was fascinated with the lifestyle of the Wampanoag tribe
and decided to interpret a typical home with available materials. Students
who are intrigued by an aspect of their classroom curriculum or by a book
they are reading often expand the experience in their artwork. Those who are
not enamored of classroom topics are not required to relive the uninteresting
curriculum during their art class, as can happen with whole-class interdisci-
plinary art projects.

School-Appropriate Subject Matter

Learner-directed artwork occasionally reflects questionable visual culture
experienced by children. Discuss appropriate and inappropriate subject matter for your school community. In the very public art classroom, certain controversial topics such as violence and weapons might cause problems for both
student and teacher. In this case, students are encouraged to explore those
topics in the privacy of their home art studio. Most students will appreciate
an open and honest class discussion about these issues.

Letting go of control of subject matter can be very scary for teachers.
Don't get discouraged. There will be good days and better days. When someone does something wonderful, stop the entire class and show everyone what
has been discovered. Your approval and excitement will have a huge impact.

Sidebar 5.1. Kid Culture

When I first began teaching, I saw children's ideas in the light of the little toys that they would bring to school. Their teacher would say to them, "Put that out in your backpack and leave it at home. You are in school now." I felt that a lot of teaching was telling children to forgo their ideas, passions, and obsessions. Teaching for artistic behavior explicitly encourages students to use these sources as subject matter for their artmaking. "What do you think about when you first wake in the morning? That just might be what you will paint about, draw about, and make sculptures about." Children's subject matter must be invited into the art classroom from the very first week. Some of the things children are excited about are of no interest to adults but that is not a problem for teaching. My fascination is in how they can find a way to express these passions.

Although commercialism has a strong hold on our children, this does not mean that they lack a culture. Influenced as it is by mass media, it is still the culture they embrace; although adults might see it as tacky or exploitative, children do not. For better or worse, teachers can use those interests as the hook to connect them with artmaking. I have taught paper sculpture methods for making solid geometric shapes for years. The year I mentioned that the rectangular prism might be a good size for a stuffed animal bed, children's eyes lit up. My students are now experts at constructing rectangular prisms. By valuing students' passions and accepting their taste while exposing them to bits of ours, we create a climate of respect and build confidence.

—K. Douglas (2004a)

MORE AND LESS

By midyear, students are charging ahead and wanting more and more materials, choices, and space. An amazing discovery by a child leads to other students wanting to try the same thing. Reserve additional table space and materials as needed. Students come up with great ideas that threaten to outgrow available time and space and teacher energy. It is difficult to say no to such enthusiasm. Remember, especially in the first year, to avoid doing too much all at once, leading to teacher burnout.

In the beginning, less is more. If most students are productively occupied, it may not be the time to open any new studio centers. Teachers need to consciously limit what they introduce to students. Focus on materials and concepts that do not require your interference once students have mastered the basics. Many teacher-directed lessons are no longer useful because they require too much teacher input in the independent studio centers.

If centers are well organized and choices kept manageable, you will have adequate time to make observations and notes, intervene with struggling students, and identify trends and future needs of each class. One teacher's system is described in Sidebar 5.2. Permit yourself to teach small, without overdoing, so you have time to breathe, observe, and reflect. These children will be your students for several years; you do not have to cover everything in the first year. Be good to yourself and avoid exhaustion. One of the best parts of teaching for artistic behavior is sitting down and making art with students or having extended conversations about art and life—all too rare pleasures in the busy teacher's schedule.

Sidebar 5.2. Play and Care

In discussing his Play/Care curriculum, John Crowe (2002b) comments, "My mission was to make a dramatic point about artistic behavior. It was my opinion that my students needed to really play and truly care." Play and Care became themes for a choice-based elementary art curriculum developed by Crowe, based on his observations of student behaviors. Small-group discussions expanded on the significance of these two themes and informed Crowe as he developed goals for the program. Drawing, painting, and sculpture were explored separately with one focus in each of the first three terms. The first five weeks of each term were devoted to playing with materials and ideas, and the second five weeks emphasized caring about the work. In the fourth term, students could elect to work in any of the three areas.

Students maintained portfolios, indicating their favorite works with a star. Crowe insisted that works containing mistakes also be included in the portfolios. Ultimately, students discovered that mistakes often led to sustained activities during the "care" portion of the class. Crowe (2002b) concluded:

> So many of my classroom management problems disappeared when students could pace and direct themselves. Students could hop from one center to another in a single session, or work week after week on a major undertaking. But above all, students were required to find their own paths and delighted in the freedom to pursue them.

In order to assess student work with a caring and holistic system, Crowe adopted the symbols of hand, mind, and heart to represent the levels of artists' investment. As each term came to an end, students filled out self-evaluations based on the hand/mind/heart assessment. Parents appreciated the simplicity of the new grading system, with the hand/mind/heart symbols appearing in place of traditional assessments.

CHAPTER 6

Exhibitions

*Students are quite capable of curating their own exhibitions. When they exhibit
their own art, they view it in an entirely new context through the eyes, minds, and
hearts of others. This gives the work a dimension and quality
they would otherwise never experience.*
(Burton & McGraw, 2001, p. 31)

Whether you plan to mount a large schoolwide art show or display student
work in the art room, consider both the audience and purpose of the exhibit.
Is it a celebration of learning, a teaching display, or advocacy tool? Who will
see the exhibit? What benefits will the artists derive from participating in the
exhibit? How can you best promote your school's art program while honoring the artists and educating the school community?

Interpretive exhibits emphasize process and concepts equally with finished
products, reflecting the philosophy of teaching for artistic behavior. Work is
displayed along with artist statements and reflections, photos of young artists at
work and quotes from well-known adult artists on their own artistic behaviors
and processes. Looping videos of the art classroom in action and slide presentations enliven interpretive shows. Students help curate the exhibit, deciding on
the arrangement of works by grade, subject, theme, or medium.

WHY EXHIBIT?

Why do artists choose to show their work? Exhibition lets artists receive
feedback and communicate ideas with viewers. Some artists exhibit in order
to sell their work. Others use exhibition deadlines as an incentive to complete
a body of work. Our students are no different, exhibiting for recognition or
the reward of compliments. Many find that the school art show motivates
them to engage in greater depth. A small number of students prefer not to
exhibit at all.

In the public arena of school, students share their work with one another, much as adult artists do when they share studio space. Artists gain

insight and grow through the observations of others. Informal sharings are balanced by displays within the art room, around school, and at all-school events. Some teachers display student pieces outside the school in the community.

Students have a lot to say visually. When their teacher acknowledges this by preparing an exhibit, students know they are respected as artists. Children's artwork is elevated by thoughtful display of the work in an organized setting. Students who take an active part in creating the art exhibit become more invested in viewing the show with their families. The responsibility of planning an art show gives students confidence and ownership. Including student perspectives insures that the show will be culturally relevant to the artist participants. After all, who knows best how to appeal to the interests of children?

THE ARTIST STATEMENT

Choice-based exhibits are distinguished by the addition of artist statements accompanying each piece. These are comments directly supplied by the artist and address concept, technique, or personal relevancy. Students are invited to supply information that the viewer wouldn't know about their work. These statements are a window into the artist's thinking and provide background information which encourages prolonged viewing. Cynthia Bencal, an elementary principal, enjoys reading artist statements at the exhibit because she learns so much about the children in her school.

Scribes help young children prepare their artist statements by writing down their words. Older students join parents in conversing with the children and transcribing what they say. Sample questions include:

- Tell me about your work.
- What do you want people to notice?
- Where did you find this idea?
- How did you make this?

Some teachers tape-record statements to transcribe later, or type as the child dictates. A good plan is to edit, print, and trim statements right away and attach them directly to each artwork.

The following artist statements contrast the egocentric thinking dictated by a kindergarten girl with figurative language written by a fifth grader. From each of these statements, the viewer gains insight into the artist's thinking and problem solving. Kindergartner Hannah is searching for a meaningful idea to pursue at the clay center:

This is me. I am sitting on a throne. When I was at the clay tabl started to think about what to do. And I was going to make a kin then I thought: Why make a king when I can make me sitting on throne?

Katherine, a fifth-grader and an experienced clay sculptor, considers the viewer as she personifies her dragon:

My artwork, a medium-sized clay figure, is splashed about with red and gold paint. A ridge of black clay spikes adorns the tail of the tiny sculpted figure, created from a lump of lifeless clay. The eyes glow out like coals as it sits quietly on the table while humans walk by gawking at it.

Artist statements reveal a great deal about the artist, artistic behaviors, and values. Writing about one's own art is satisfying.

A third-grade classroom teacher uses art show pieces as writing prompts. This results in rich artist statements created outside of art class. More often students write their statements during art class, and additional time must be allotted for this purpose. A small center can be set up with paper, pens, and glue sticks. Artist statements are powerful evidence of the deep learning in a choice-based art education. Once you start including them, you will never want to leave them out of an exhibit.

YEAR-ROUND EXHIBITS

Within the art room, where can student work be displayed? Are there bulletin boards or wires stretched across the room where artwork can be attached? Can students display their work from week to week? It is important to think about whose work will be on display. Those students who need a morale boost will benefit by seeing their work up on the wall. A group of fifth-grade boys managed one bulletin board, adding their new work as it evolved over the year. Younger students eagerly anticipated new work by the older artists. Individual centers are broadened with the inclusion of a student display. Keep a digital camera handy to take photos of exemplary work before it leaves the classroom. A display of printed photos or web display will inform others of the many possibilities within each center.

Around your school, there are likely and unlikely places to display art. The principal's office and main office provide great visibility for the art program. Artwork hung in cafeterias, auditoriums, and school lobbies enhances school culture.

Thematic Displays

Certain themes emerge in children's art. Develop a limited exhibit around one of these themes and invite students to participate during an introductory demonstration. When shows include a wide age range, viewers note developmental stages in artmaking. Some examples of thematic exhibits include the human figure, animals, landscape, and artwork inspired by literature.

Art Shows on the Internet

Showing your school art exhibit on the Internet has some great benefits for program advocacy. Often the show can stay up for a number of years. Plate 6.1 shows one layout of a class art exhibit. Distant family members can view student work while students experience being published online. Art exhibits bring increased traffic to school Web sites. Districts have various policies regarding online display of student work so it is important to understand and follow those guidelines.

Art Shows in Your District

Art teachers are frequently asked to make displays within their school system. This show will be seen by many administrators and teachers, as well as parents. It is a perfect venue to explain about teaching for artistic behavior. Select artwork showing a variety of media and approaches and be sure to include artist statements and information on choice practice, philosophy, and standards.

Art Shows in the Community

Community arts councils are often happy to include school exhibits with their festivals and special events (see Plate 6.2). Here is another visibility opportunity where students can be recognized for their fine ideas. Art from a school exhibit is shown in the larger community without much additional preparation. Communicate clearly with community groups about their goals and yours. Prizes and competitions create problems, so issues need to be clarified in advance. If you decide to involve your program in a community event, plan promotion so families and administrators are aware of your efforts beyond the classroom.

All-School Art Shows

For artists and art teachers alike, exhibitions present a paradox of excitement and dread, pride and anxiety. Open up the process to students, allowing for choice, reflection, and, ultimately, ownership. It may seem overwhelming to give up control of the show's content to students, but the results will be very exciting. Students can identify themes, promote schoolwide interest in the show, and plan for the exhibition areas. Student curators maintain the exhibit, making certain that everyone's artwork is safely displayed. When students feel invested in the art show, this is conveyed to their families, resulting in strong parental support for choice-based art education. Students are our best allies!

INTEGRATING EXHIBITS INTO THE SCHOOL CURRICULUM

If your in-school art show hangs in the hallways for more than a few days, it can become integrated into learning at your school. Students visit the show as an in-school field trip with the focus provided by the art teacher and supported by classroom teachers. Sidebar 6.1 (on the following page) is a sample letter to classroom teachers inviting them to bring their students to the exhibit. These teachers use the exhibit for descriptive paragraph prompts and letter-writing lessons. Teachers create graphic organizers for students to fill out during their viewing of the show. Some students write fan letters to their favorite artists (see Plate 6.3) and some of the artists write back! The school art show creates an organic learning opportunity that is accessed by teachers in many ways.

Sidebar 6.1. In-School Field Trip

Teachers appreciate information on upcoming art exhibits in the school. This is a flier that appeared in teacher mailboxes the day before an elementary school spring show:

> No permission slips to collect!
> No bag lunches to pack!
> No long rides in a noisy bus!

Grade 3 students welcome you to an exhibit of their chosen work. The middle floor has been transformed into a gallery of paintings, prints, drawings, collages, masks, puppets, weaving, and sculpture. When artists visit museums and galleries they take various approaches to viewing. Some look to see what their friends have been making or subject matter that interests them. Others look at artworks done with materials that attract them, still others prefer to be surprised by something new or intriguing.

If your schedule permits time to visit the exhibit in small or large groups, you may find these favorites can serve as stimulus for descriptive writing, letter writing to an artist, or as the starting point for verbal discussion. Questions and answers about things that students see encourage deeper thinking and more careful looking. Some artworks are accompanied by artist statements, which help us all look more carefully. The artists have generously consented to leaving their work here until the end of the month. We look forward to your visit and your feedback!

—Mrs. Douglas and the children of Grade 3

Studio Centers

In Part II, we highlight both instruction and materials management issues that are unique to choice-based teaching. Studio centers organize and make explicit the range of choices available to students.

Drawing, painting, collage, and sculpture provide basic media choices for students. With these centers, the choice-based classroom could be considered complete. The first three chapters in Part II explore these centers in depth. Most choice-based classrooms contain other important centers, including printmaking, clay, and fiber arts. There are many additional possibilities for studio centers. Ephemeral studio centers, which appear briefly, and smaller centers are addressed in Chapter 11, including book arts, digital arts, mask making, puppetry, architecture, and murals. Some teachers fold these choices into larger centers: for instance, mask making could be embedded with sculpture. The number of specific centers you create depends upon your teaching space and resources, ages of your students, your schedule, and your particular skills and interests.

The first time a studio center appears in your classroom or on your traveling cart, it is important to demonstrate three things: what students will find there, how to use it, and how materials will be put away. Observe and take notes as you watch your students in a new center. Note if there is a need for modifying your demonstrations or adjusting the design of the studio center for improved student understandings.

For students new to choice-based learning it is essential to open each studio center with the simplest materials. It is also important to open centers in a certain sequence. Begin with drawing, then simple painting, followed by collage, for the first three classes. If students have trouble with management or cleanup, slow the opening of additional centers. Offer incentives of new choices when you observe productive work and efficient cleanup. The promise of additional materials and more choices is an inspiring and authentic reward.

As time passes, you will spiral back through the studio centers, gradually adding more complicated materials, such as liquid tempera to the paint center or plaster at the sculpture table. These new materials are introduced through the 5-minute demo. If you observe problems with work in a particular center, review the issues with students. Needs will vary from class to class and can be addressed by customizing your demos. A well-organized plan book is essential for this.

CHAPTER 7

Drawing

Like many children and young people, I attempted to write poetry, which sooner or later I tore up. I can remember that drawing released me from this condition, that is, that it let me live outside of time and space, so that I no longer felt myself.
(Kandinsky, 1964, p. 27)

INTRODUCTION TO THE DRAWING CENTER

What Do Artists Draw?

Artists make artwork about the things that are churning in their minds. Students are thinking hard about a lot of things that are important to them, some of which appear in their drawings. The following list is found in Pauline Joseph's classroom, hanging in the drawing studio center.

Artists Draw:

- What they see
- What they remember
- What they imagine
- What they feel
- Marks with a drawing tool

Shallow boxes filled with basic drawing materials, including pencils, colored pencils, erasers, markers, and crayons along with templates and rulers, are ready at the tables. Students are invited to explore these materials and create the sort of drawing that they like to make. Some students set a horse or dinosaur model in front of their paper and begin an observational drawing, while others may be scribbling, enchanted by the marks on paper.

The phrase *scribble stage* describes beginning efforts at all centers in the choice-based art program. It sets apart those who are novices from those who have more experience with a particular medium. Readers may be familiar with

Viktor Lowenfeld's (Lowenfeld & Brittain, 1957) description of the scribbling stages of development:

> In the first stages of scribbling no other stimulation is necessary except the encouragement of the teacher to go ahead with the activity. As has been said before, scribbling should not be interfered with. This rule is important for the first as well as for the later stages, since such interference would not only deprive the child of vital experiences, but would also inhibit him in his further work. Interferences, like the one mentioned, in which adults cannot soon enough see representations that are related to reality, may interrupt the growth of the child's motor activities in the same way as forcing the child to scribble with the right hand, when he prefers to use the left. (p. 93)

Developmental disparities occur with all age groups. Take note of *what* is being drawn more than *how* it is being drawn. In future classes, demos will address the expansion of skills in drawing and other media. The most important thing to offer in the first week is time, space, and a safe environment for all to reengage in their own artwork. Many children have been drawing at home and welcome the invitation to continue this work in art class. Third-grader Kelsey's sketchbook traveled with her throughout the year:

> I get my sketch diary and then I'll get my crayons from my closet. I always use the 64 pack. If I am tired of horses or ballerinas, I will think of something and try it. If it doesn't come out good, I'll keep it anyway and just keep trying to draw it. Sometimes I'll look at pictures and I try to copy. The more I try the better the picture looks. I chose the dogs for the art show because they are really cute. I chose the horses because I drew them when I was 5. I chose the dancers because the ballerinas look like they are popping out of the page.

Resources for Drawing

Art room bookshelves offer visual dictionaries and encyclopedias, atlases, discarded science books, and calendars showing cars, nature, and other topics of interest. Boxes of art postcards stimulate ideas for artworks as well. How-to drawing books are available for children's use. Some teachers discourage drawing books, feeling strongly that a prescribed method of drawing may damage a child's inner sensitivity. However, certain children find these books helpful while others ignore the books and employ their own drawing strategies. Toys, models, and natural objects displayed around the room are available for closer inspection. Sidebar 7.1 describes some interactions between students, teachers, and drawing challenges.

Sidebar 7.1. Resources for Learning

Nan Hathaway (2005) relies on resources to challenge her students at the Drawing Center. On the first day of art class, she tells students about the various available references:

> I point out the Image File, which is a box of pictures that artists refer to when they need visual information. I have placed several drawing books in this center as well, along with art reproductions and examples of children's drawings. There is also a box of models, consisting of plastic dinosaurs, real shells, fossils and animals, both wild and domestic. There is also an artist's wooden figure and a model of a human skeleton, all tools of the trade. During the first day of class, I look around and see students drawing from models, from photographs, from the wooden figure, and from each other. Students ask me questions, such as "Where does a person's shoulder attach?" or "Do you have a picture of a rocket I could see?" We go online to NASA for some technical information. Idea books and portfolios are started. One student tells me he has the idea of a raft in his head, which would hold his sister and him. He makes visual notes about it in his idea book. Another student gathers a large menagerie of animals and sets out to draw each one on her portfolio cover. A discovery is made by one student of a new art process: If you first draw with a gold paint pen, then draw over it with a marker, the gold ink resists the marker, and shines through. Some students stop their own work to admire the result. This prompts a discussion involving two other students, about how they remember using oil pastels and watercolor for an oil resist last year, and wax crayon and paint for a wax resist in Sunday school. These students are 5 and 6 years old. These students are artists.

EXPANDED DRAWING

What kinds of artworks emerge at the drawing center? Each class will have its own unique culture with drawing enthusiasts who pursue a multitude of topics. Drawing students are very aware of visual culture and often bring their favorite books and visual references to class. Those who are most committed to drawing often attract followers. Cohort groups develop around subject matter or style, such as superheroes and Manga. As the year unfolds, the teacher challenges students with more materials and techniques appropriate to developmental levels and actively searches for new and exciting images to inspire new drawings. The following examples of new media, techniques, and approaches suggest a few of the many ways for drawing to expand.

New Drawing Media and Techniques

Pen and ink, pastels, and charcoal add variation to students' graphic possibilities. Children who do not specialize in drawing may be attracted to new drawing materials and techniques. Demos on texture, tone, and shading provide incentives to develop skills with these more unusual materials. Teaching for artistic behavior invites instructors to improvise solutions for the best use of artistic media. Charcoal and pastels are organized in special containers to keep them separate from all other drawing materials. Ink bottles must be supported to avoid spills; Plate 7.1 shows a teacher-designed structure to hold ink so students can focus on their drawing. These drawing media may need their own space to keep the mess confined. With forethought, learners can use these tempting materials successfully without close supervision.

Spatial Representation

Depth is an illusion and artists are masterful illusionists! "How can you make objects on a flat surface such as paper appear three-dimensional?" students are asked. Children develop their own conventions to indicate space, convincing to the viewer and satisfactory to the artist. As drawing skills advance, children seek more sophisticated methods to show distance. Knowledge of foreground, middle ground, and background is useful in composing a picture. Using examples, students can see how a horizon line establishes the position of objects in their drawing. Overlaps indicate proximity of objects to one another. The picture plane establishes space; items lower on the picture plane appear closer to the viewer. These elements are included in a drawing demonstration, with greater complexity added for older students. Spatial understanding is developmental and not everyone will pick up these techniques at the same time. Children watch each other at work and the concept is reinforced. Eventually, others begin to incorporate these ideas in their own work.

Demos on perspective drawing enliven older students who may already be familiar with its look while not yet knowing how to do it. Students at all ages may try to mimic perspective drawing, but understanding it is developmental. Wait until you see evidence of students using perspective in their own drawings. Make sure they are ready.

Observation Drawing

Children enjoy learning to draw objects that appeal to them. In one classroom an old bicycle sits on the counter by the drawing center. Behind it hang diagrams, photographs, and drawings of bicycles. The teacher reminds children that some things can be drawn from memory, but other objects require close observation for accuracy. The bicycle is one of those things. Using a large paper and a crayon, the teacher sketches familiar shapes: two circles for the wheels, the triangular bars connecting them, and then other parts connected to the handlebars. The sketch is very simple. Children are challenged to draw the bicycle and hang their finished drawings on the bulletin board. Soon the board is very full, and it is fascinating to see all the drawing styles and approaches to solving the problem. Younger students get interested and add their bicycle drawings to the display. Some children note the differences in accuracy of the drawings. This opens a discussion of how people's ability to see and draw improves with age and practice. This observation drawing experience can be applied to any engaging objects and could even include still life drawing.

Cartoons, Comic Books, and Graphic Novels

Five fifth-grade boys sit down one afternoon to continue their work on an action comic book with many superheroes. These boys have been drawing together for several years during art class. They are discussing elements that contribute to a story line. Each character must be explored through a map of the person's world, including where he lives, his allies and enemies, his special skills and powers, and his personality. Mastering the character requires drawing good expressions, with a strong or "buff" body and careful attention paid to its shape. The story line must be clear, funny, and have action. Since many hands work on the cartoon, the boys note that it should be quick to draw. Action is depicted with words such as *Pow!* and *Whoosh!* Action lines around characters help to suggest movement. The boys purposely have no big ending to their comic books, so the series can continue if they choose to follow up at a later date. Plate 7.2 shows a cartoon cohort discussing their work.

Cartoons, comic books, and graphic novels are a great source of entertainment, both for creators and readers. Groups of children enjoy working together, developing a story line, and designing characters and personalities. The same narrative may carry over from one comic to another or may change over time. How do you know if your students are learning while working together on comics? Determine important objectives and watch for their growth: cooperative work, planning, storytelling, writing, and character development. For some members of the group, drawing may be secondary to these valuable life skills.

ENCOURAGING GROWTH

To a great extent, students teach themselves to draw. The teacher keeps individuals moving forward so that drawings show growth over time. The core group of students who frequent the drawing center require very little other than basic materials and references. Their discussions may become heated, but almost always the talk is focused on their work. Listen carefully before you intervene. David, in grade 2, is a self-propelled learner who gets others involved in his plan:

> When I was in first grade, my friend made a dragon and I really liked it. Then I drew my own dragon and kept making it bigger and bigger and stronger so it looks alive. I read a lot of books about dragons once I got interested. I found out that if I want to draw a lot of dragons, I need more people to help. These giant dragons would take me a lot of time if I had to do it by myself. Each week, I take the dragons home and then I bring them back to art class.

This chapter gives but a few of the many possible approaches to teach and expand upon drawing. The broad topics selected for inclusion have proven to be successful for independent learning. The teacher may choose to demo gesture or contour drawing or any other drawing methods, if need for this instruction surfaces in the classroom. Responsive teachers observe what students need and adjust accordingly. This is how emergent curriculum develops in choice-based art education.

CHAPTER 8

Painting

*Each distinctive painter has his own brush dance. Seurat, surprisingly, has a kind
of fox-trot, Manet a waltz. Berthe Morisot you might say is almost a figure skater,
skating and jumping and twirling. De Kooning includes almost every tempo—
very slow and very fast, very happy and very blue, all within a single picture.*
(Thiebaud, 2000, pp. 49–50)

WAKING UP THE PAINTS

Children embrace painting in a variety of ways, but many dive in with delight,
fascinated with liquid movement on dry or wet paper, with the marks made by
different brushes and by the magical changes one color makes in combination
with another. Once the painting studio center is open, students have the opportunity to paint whenever they want. Tables are set up with soft brushes, watercolor boxes, coffee cans filled halfway with water, sponges, and thick white
construction paper. A painting smock rests on the back of each chair. The
teacher demonstrates how to wake up the watercolors with water and how to
keep brushes clean by rinsing them and wiping them on the sponge when they
change colors. Students are encouraged to discover what happens when colors
are mixed on the paper or in palettes. Paper surfaces are discussed, with emphasis on heavier paper for paints. White construction paper is quite absorbent and
helps colors stay bright even when layered. Students may choose to paint or
continue with the drawing materials that they used during the previous class.

Toward the end of the first painting class, the teacher shows children where
to put their signed work, how to clean brushes, rinse out their water cans, and
hang up their smocks. Reminders to those working at other centers ensure that
materials there have also been put away properly.

Setting Up a Painting Space

Early in the school year, the demonstration focuses on how to set up a
painting space. All materials are carefully arranged next to the painter's domi-
nant hand for easy reach. It is a good idea to provide enough supplies so that

nobody has to share or reach over. In the early weeks, the painting center may be very popular and more space will be necessary. When possible, cover additional tables with newspaper and expand the center. If everyone must fit at one area, students can start out with smaller paper. As more centers open up, the flow will even off, allowing children to work on large painting surfaces if they choose.

Resources

The painting menu lists materials that students must set up before they can paint. The order is critical to the setup procedure. Pictures inform non-readers of the routine.

1. Smock or apron
2. Water can or cup
3. Brushes
4. Sponge (to wipe excess water off brush)
5. Palette
6. Choice of paint
7. Thick paper

Color wheels are posted permanently in the painting center for those who find them helpful. Vocabulary words such as *primary, complementary,* and *tint* are illustrated with paint swatches. Exemplars of varied painting genres by both adult and child artists hang overhead. Landscapes, cityscapes, still lifes, portraits, and abstract and expressionist paintings inspire students to identify with their preferred style.

Color Mixing

When things are going smoothly in the painting center, it is time to set out tempera paints. This paint is ideal for color mixing and invites a demonstration with paint palettes. Children are expected to mix all their own colors, blending paints to please themselves. Upon seeing a newly invented color, a student observes out loud, "Wow, look at that army green!" The teacher comments, "Look how that red stands out next to the green color you mixed." Another child asks, "What colors did you mix to get that skin color?" Sharing amazing discoveries shows color theory in action without having to demonstrate it. Students like third-grader Sarah share their techniques and color discoveries with classmates:

> First, I was trying to make it look like a sky painting but then I added some other colors. I took paint and put it over it. Then I took sgraffito

sticks and I scraped some of the paint off of it. The paintbrushes had some paint on them and I dabbed them on the paper. I took all kinds of colors and mixed them all up together on the palette. My most favorite color was the sky color.

Color wheels are useful tools for inquisitive artists, but for many painters, including children, color is intuitive. Students who paint often become aware of fine nuances in color and develop skills that serve them well later in the year. By experimenting and playing with paint, young artists learn how saturated colors can evolve into tints, tones, and shades.

After liquid tempera paint is introduced, watercolor sets remain out and cake temperas are also available. Individual cakes can fit into shallow cardboard boxes, offering a variety of colors. Some painters prefer these to the liquid tempera, as they are less messy yet still provide brilliant color. Teachers gently remind painters about wiping brushes, utilizing the mixing palettes, and keeping colors clean, encouraging students to develop routines. Even if children are too young to learn this, they each have their own paint tray and can paint with their own mud. Children become aware of their color preferences and consistently mix the colors that they need. Just as there is not one correct way to paint, there is no one right way to teach painting. Each of us develops our own preferred method of selecting and setting up paints and painting routines.

Student Management of the Painting Center

Organized cleanup routines make painting doable for even the shortest class periods. At the end of the first painting class, children gather for another demonstration. From the setup menu, students see that painting materials are put away starting at the bottom of the list. This results in paintings being put away to dry first. Then paint trays are stacked on counters and sponges go in a basket on the table. Dirty palettes and brushes soak in a large tub and water cans are emptied at the sink. Last, smocks and aprons are hung up to dry. Following the menu with teacher reinforcement, children can manage without jams or spills at the sink. As time allows, older students can wash their brushes; the teacher washes brushes and palettes quickly for younger students. The children are proud to take responsibility for the painting center, and it is a great bonus for their teacher.

DISCOVERY LEARNING

With no assigned subject matter, students are free to experiment with the paint as long as they wish. This scribble stage of painting involves lots of color investigation, mixing up nearly every color imaginable. Layering on thick paint, trying the biggest and smallest brush possible, and then scraping, wiping, crumpling, and folding the paper are all part of discovery. Unsuccessful attempts become subject for discussion: Was the paper too thin? The brush too wide? The rinsing water too dirty? Through exploration, students learn by using the paint in a way that is effective for them.

Young painters often start with nonobjective compositions, full of purpose and meaning to the artist. Sometimes these paintings record color discoveries. Celebrating the energy and beauty of nonobjective work helps children and adults appreciate this aesthetic. By sharing the work of artists such as Kandinsky or Frankenthaler, teachers show that there is much more to painting than literal narratives.

Early painting demonstrations focus on the opacity of the paint and the *no fear factor*. After mixing colors in the palette, the teacher puts an unattractive splotch in the corner of the painting. Getting upset and pretending to throw the paper away, the teacher hams it up. Children point out that the paint is opaque and can cover the offending mark. The words NO FEAR are written on the painting chart. When fear of mistakes is taken away, children become free with the brush and more experimental. Encourage students to practice making mistakes and then fixing them.

EXPANDED PAINTING

When students around the room are working effectively, the teacher has the pleasure of instructing small groups in greater depth. The Five-Minute Museum, introduced in Chapter 3, is a good way to highlight genres of painting. Over three classes, the Museum addresses subject matter, style, and a bit of art history, using three different sets of paintings (see Plate 3.1). Of course, the same can be done at other times for other studio centers. This whole-group demo motivates a smaller group interested in learning more.

Painting Cohorts

Interested painters join their teacher around the demonstration table while the rest of the class goes to other studio centers. The teacher begins on 2' x 3' heavy paper, modeling one way to start a painting. Large areas are blocked in with slightly tinted water and gradually more paint is added. Children who like to paint this large agree to work on the piece for three or more art classes. Be aware that it may take longer for ideas to surface in painting versus drawing. Drawing media has been used by children since preschool, but paint is less familiar. As children mature, subject matter becomes more important to them in their paintings. Stimulated by the large reproductions in the Five-Minute Museum, painters like Chris bring their interests and ideas into their paintings:

> This is my painting of Fenway Park. I painted this because I like base-ball, I like going to games, and I like watching games on TV. I like when you mess up with paint because you can just paint over it. This painting is my favorite and I spent about 4 weeks working on it. When I watch TV, I look at the fields, and then when I come to art I know what to put in my painting.

Some children paint large only once, returning thereafter to the usual 12" x 18" paper. Others are transformed by the freedom of working with big arm motion and kinesthetic movements.

The painting cohort gathers together at the next class to discuss how to change mistakes, cover bare paper, and add texture and details. Students working in landscape are given laminated reproductions ranging from the Fauves to the Florida Highwaymen to Hockney. Here they find multiple solutions to problems of sky and horizon. The same reference help is available to portrait painters, still-life artists, and so on. By the third class, many painters begin to slow down and appreciate the leisurely pace. Students announce that they have been thinking about their paintings during the week and are pleased to reencounter them. Others totally redo their paintings; new ideas have come to them and they happily paint out large portions of the space with the thick opaque paint.

Painters often work standing up and move around the paper, stretching their arms to make the marks that they like. The beauty of the brushstrokes becomes apparent to many of them resulting in layered and very painterly work. As these layers build up, the tempera paint loses its bland flatness and colors begin to glow.

Acrylics

Older students are ready to handle a more sophisticated paint medium and look forward to the arrival of acrylic paints. Setup remains the same as for tempera, except that artists paint on gessoed cardboard or canvas board. They squeeze their paints onto cardboard palettes and blend their colors with plastic knives. A great deal of mixing goes on before any paint touches the canvas. The paint's properties are intriguing to students like fifth-grader Winston:

I like how my painting compares the daytime sun to the darkness of night. I chose acrylics since many other paints, like watercolor, can't look as unique as acrylic. If you look carefully you will see that the yellow part of the rainbow on the right is missing; its place has been taken by the moon.

Young painters become very quiet and serious while painting with acrylics. They accept the responsibility with pride because they know that adults paint with the same materials. Students commit at least three classes to their acrylic painting. As with tempera, some students continue many weeks on the same composition while others revise each week, layering new colors over previous attempts. A range of brushes is available, though some prefer to work entirely with a palette knife. Those who seek realism in their work are pleased that the paints enable them to add small details in critical areas, enhancing the overall appearance of the painting. After years of working with tempera, students stretch as painters with this new medium.

PAINTING IS IDEAL FOR CHOICE-BASED TEACHING AND LEARNING

Teaching painting is often a struggle for art teachers because of time, space, and materials management. In the choice-based learning environment, interested students take responsibility for materials and their paintings. Groups are small so students can work on large paper, enjoy a variety of tools, and work at their own speed. Artistic behaviors greatly vary; some painters work spontaneously while others sketch first (see Plate 8.1). Painting is an essential experience for young children; teaching for artistic behavior makes it doable even with large classes.

CHAPTER 9

Moving Into Three Dimensions

All sculptors must be interested in this three-dimensional aspect otherwise they'd be something else—designers or pattern-makers. It's the difference between being a painter and a sculptor. Being a sculptor means that you are living in this three-dimensional world and that's what makes it exciting. You must be discovering the whole time. A sculptor wants to know what a thing is like from the top and from beneath—a bird's eye view and a worm's eye view. It's infinite.

(Moore, 1986, p. 79)

Certain children are concrete three-dimensional thinkers caught in the two-dimensional paper world of the school environment. These children are thirsty for sculpture work in a paper and pencil desert! They are inventors, engineers, scientists, mathematicians, designers, and architects whose discoveries inspire both kinetic and stationary constructions at the sculpture center. Often students who have had issues with behavior, or can't sit still, or get frustrated easily with other art forms gain great confidence at the sculpture center. Before moving directly to three-dimensional art, students first learn about collage and paper sculpture techniques.

COLLAGE

The collage center is one of the first studio centers to open. On this grand opening day, three tables each contain a shallow box of paper shapes and another of collage tools and materials. The introduction to the collage center focuses on

- High-quality scissors and scissors that cut patterned edges
- Paper punches
- Brass fasteners
- String

- White school glue
- Paper in varied colors, weights, and textures

Students are encouraged to play around with collage, making varied edges by cutting and tearing paper. Collage artists overlap shapes for contrast; layers give a semblance of depth. After deciding upon a composition, students glue the pieces down. Plate 9.1 shows a student's collage in response to a class demo on the human figure.

Some students work exclusively at one studio center each class, others move from area to area, taking their work with them. Mixed-media artwork includes collages illuminated with paint and drawings embellished with collaged shapes. Students' collage work benefits by good organization. Clear boxes containing paper are labeled by color and type (shiny, patterned, and transparent) to make it simple for children to find the just-right paper for their work. Adam is an artist in the third grade who has strong feelings about his materials:

> You can make a collage by taking a piece of paper and cutting it out in any way without needing to draw any lines. With collage, you can make small shapes and you can make really big ones. A pencil or crayon or marker changes the color of the paper when you draw with them and you might not like how the color turns out. When you pick a certain color paper, you can't change the color—it always stays the same. You can make very detailed pictures with collage and it can take a long time but it is worth it in the end.

The collage and sculpture centers are good neighbors because they build similar skills using many of the same tools and materials. Plate 2.2 shows an organized studio center for both collage and sculpture work. Routines must be in place for the transition from two-dimensional to three-dimensional work because sculpture requires far more materials and space. Paper sculpture is a good segue into three-dimensional thinking.

PAPER SCULPTURE

When students design paper collages, three-dimensional elements often emerge in their work. Adding dispensers of clear tape to the supply boxes facilitates students' ability to add dimension with paper. The demonstration shows a few simple ways to make the paper stand up and connect to other paper, but the rest is up to the children. All sorts of great things happen:

hats, forts, houses, and jewelry suddenly appear. Some learners spend most of the class punching holes in the paper and trying out the brass fasteners. New tools are exciting and deserve practice! Paper forms can be embellished with paint or marker. Children move easily around the room to find what they need to finish their work. If you think about it, moving from one thing to another comes very naturally to children. It is we teachers who tend to get uneasy when we can't predict or manage every student move.

Attachments

Can you envision a challenge among student sculptors to see how many fastening techniques they can come up with and then displaying the results? One teacher established an attachment test for students, likening it to the deep-water swim test. Students must demonstrate three different means of attaching three varied materials together, using no adhesives. Successful completion of the attachment test results in access to tape and glue throughout the year. Students rise to this type of challenge because it is fun with desirable outcomes.

Tape and Glue. Some connections work better with glue and some work better with tape or other materials. Tape is the one adhesive that provides students the greatest possibilities for improvisation. Without tape, many creative opportunities are discarded due to the limitations of glue. It will be necessary to teach young children how to cut tape without hurting themselves on the serrated edge of the dispensers. For attachments better suited for glue, remind children to use minimal amounts for best results—glue can't stick when it is still wet.

Wire and Fasteners. Wire and pipe cleaners are especially good for connecting foam and plastic, which do not attach well with glue or tape. Brass fasteners connect paper and cardboard, permitting pieces to move independently.

Fibers. Some students find success in sewing objects together with a big needle and yarn. Wrapping or tying with ribbon, yarn, or string is another option, and your students will come up with even more possibilities.

Hot Glue. Older students can be trained to safely use a low-temperature glue gun. They use this tool for materials that defy attachment by other means. Hot glue definitely helps with some of the more exotic attachment problems. Be sure to address safety issues by limiting both time and numbers near the hot glue guns.

Supports

A class demonstration focuses on supports for upright constructions. When designing a piece with a 90-degree angle, supports are necessary. Show students how to make a brace out of a cardboard triangle. If a box is the end result, explain that once the other sides are attached, they will support the single standing wall, with or without the brace. As learners gain familiarity with structures, they improvise ways to make their sculptures strong.

As children gain ability with paper sculpture, they start making toys. Paper airplanes are a perennial part of kid culture, with the skill being passed from older to younger children. Origami-adept aeronauts and their classmates will design and fold a fleet of planes in the classroom. It is important for the teacher to manage this engagement for productive learning. After construction, planes are decorated with individual markings and then, when the weather is good, the class heads out to the playground for a test run. While paper airplanes are considered controversial by some adults because they are often associated with mischief, in teaching for artistic behavior rogue topics are leveraged for learning—in this case, about balance, weight, structure, and basic engineering.

THE SCULPTURE CENTER

> *This is a boat. It is very big. It says SS Titanic on it. It has two styrofoam plates on the bottom. I chose them because I know that styrofoam floats and now I can put it in water and it will float. I had a little trouble making it. It was hard to keep the tape on and to keep the flag staying up. Sometimes some of my art things fail. Sometimes that bothers me because I have been working hard, so I don't like to see them fail. I feel like I am getting better at building.*
>
> —Mitchell, Grade 4

Choice-based teachers look forward to the grand opening of the sculpture center with both anticipation and trepidation. This popular studio center requires vigilance to keep it running smoothly. Children like Mitchell, who have the need to construct, prowl among the supplies seeking just-right materials for their boat, house, space ship, stadium, or invention. Make sure that those materials are available in sufficient quantity by monitoring supplies near the end of each class. Indeed, it is a small trade-off in order to engage young artists in their work.

Collections

Searching for art materials and objects is a rewarding artistic behavior. Collecting objects to inspire artmaking extends the art class into the students' personal lives (Topal and Gandini, 1999). When children collect objects outside of school, they are planning and thinking about their artwork. Such collections influenced educator George Szekely (2005) to adapt his teaching practice based on his observations as described here:

> We showed respect for the children's wasp nests, erasers, bottle caps and other things they designated as collectable. My new approach to teaching art history and art appreciation through objects of interest to children was natural after meeting future collectors, curators, and preservationists at home. (p. 49)

In the classes leading up to the opening of the sculpture center, mention collections and encourage students to bring in found objects and recyclables for the art room. "If you have these things at home," the teacher suggests, "get a paper bag and find a safe place where you can keep it. Add your found objects to the bag and then bring them in for our sculpture center." Many communities have recycle centers where teachers gather quantities of manufacturers' discards. Find out if there is of one of these wonderful resources near you to supplement students' collections of found objects.

Introducing Found Objects to Sculpture

Early in the school year, sculptures should be limited in scale. This restriction forces students to concentrate on developing good habits at this center. A standard piece of cardboard (9" x 12" or smaller) is a good size limit. As students push these limits, balance what they can realistically manage with your storage options.

The sculpture center is the favorite place for many of the most active students. Here they can build objects to represent their interests, accomplishments and dreams. This area is in high demand, but it can become the teacher's nightmare. Materials require constant restocking and cleanup requires considerable attention. The trade-off is in watching genuine excitement over a new achievement and object to take home. In Plate 9.2 students work collaboratively on a long-term sculpture.

Nan Hathaway sends a letter home to families when she opens her sculptural construction center to educate them on developmental stages in three-dimensional artmaking (Sidebar 9.1). Early efforts from this center often

Sidebar 9.1. On Toilet Paper Tubes, Scotch Tape, and Strawberry Baskets

Dear Families,

Many of you are familiar with the universal developmental sequence that takes place as children begin to draw. Just as babies progress from scooting to crawling and finally to walking, children move predictably in their drawings from the scribble stage to the schematic stage to the realistic stage. It is interesting to note that making images is a universal human activity. It is also interesting that at a certain point, most people simply stop image making altogether. According to Peter London in *No More Secondhand Art* (1989), "We have learned to be embarrassed by our efforts. We have learned to feel so inept and disenfranchised from our own visual expression that we simply stop doing it altogether" (p. xiii). Perhaps, sadly, this is the last developmental stage of image making for many.

Many of us are not as familiar or comfortable with the developmental stages of three-dimensional work, yet no doubt a similar progression exists. In order to create a sculptural piece of art, students must learn a great deal about balance and support. Students discover how to attach one object to another, how to achieve height, width, and unity. Early sculptural attempts may look no more organized than a 3-year-old's scribble, but are just as necessary and valid as those early marks with crayon or marker. A great deal of learning is taking place when a student engineers a three-dimensional object. What materials are interesting and available? Should one glue, tape, staple, or lash? Which glue works best for which material? Is the hot glue gun REALLY the savior of all things 3-D? How does one support a heavy object? What surface treatment adds beauty, interest, or definition? Should the sculpture be free standing or attached to a base? Is the object functional or decorative? Many meaningful questions arise while constructing objects in art. Although the results do not always accurately reflect the importance of the process, the process has real value and is a meaningful aspect of the authentic work of artists.

I suspect those of you who house vast landscapes of structures made from cardboard, paper tubes, and pipe cleaners are pulling your hair out, wondering how to find room to store and display all this recycled . . . stuff. More importantly, you may be struggling with how to admire and validate the work your child is so proud of.

Some parents and teachers are quite savvy in talking about art with children. Instead of asking, "What IS that?" many people considerately inquire "Would you like to tell me about your picture (or sculpture or mobile or weaving)?" Some parents allow a certain spot at home for display, and when it is full, a child must select things that need to go in order to make room for new pieces. Another tactic is to agree to display a piece for a little while, and

---

Sidebar 9.1, *continued*

then take it apart in order to reuse or recycle the parts. It is not necessary to keep every object your child drags home indefinitely, and children will understand that there is simply not room for it all. While a certain period of admiration and display is welcome, much of this early sculpture is much more about process than product, and the resulting object may have relatively little importance to your child once it is complete.

In past years, on one day near the end of the school year, I would set up an Inventor's Workshop. Toilet paper tubes, scraps of Styrofoam, tape, and staples would come out, and in a flurry of excited enthusiasm, students would create something that was of importance to them. It was by far the most popular activity I facilitated. Some students waited all year for this one glorious day. It is little surprise that the "Construction Center" in the art room is the most popular workstation right now, and while the objects that leave my room are sometimes challenging for adults, it is important to recognize the significance and value of creative construction. One must learn to walk before one can run.

—Nan Hathaway (2006a, pp. 38–39)

---

appear awkward, yet students are extremely proud of their achievements. It is important to give learners ample time to practice at sculpture and to improve their skills.

Limits for Sculpture

Size specifications may increase midyear, depending upon your storage availability. Working larger encourages careful planning and organization. Students can construct in sections, which remain separate so they are easily stored. Younger students are more inclined to take their work home each week, eager to play with it after school. This alleviates issues of storage but may result in depleted supplies. Talk honestly with students about issues of supply and demand, so they realize that the items in this center need to be shared by the entire school. Everyone should help conserve materials. As students become more proficient in sculpture skills, concepts and materials become more complex.

Cleanup at the Sculpture Center

The sculpture center is constantly in disarray, due to the large volume of materials and high usage. Children must put everything away in the right places and discard tiny bits of unusable materials. As students' efforts indicate that they can manage this center, the teacher gradually adds more materials for their enjoyment.

EXPANDED SCULPTURE

If you have enough space in your sculpture center, add more material and technique choices such as wire sculpture, where students can "draw" with wire, plaster, and papier mâché. Sculptural learning integrates the scientific principles of balance, structure, and kinesthetics. Jay, a budding engineer, built parachutes for 3 years and wrote about aerodynamics in one of his artist statements:

A Parachute Needs to Have:

- Lightweight materials
- Thin string to hold the balloon
- Weight hanging from the basket so it doesn't flop
- Weights of wrapped pipe cleaners at the end of a small axle

I made parachutes last year and the year before that. I didn't know much about parachute weights and airbags on the balloon. The weight goes below the basket and has a small, long vertical axle that pulls it down. It doesn't let the balloon drag or flop down. If there was no weight, it would be just like dropping a piece of cloth. Tissue paper is ideal for the balloon because it is lightweight and can trap air. Large amounts of tissue paper can make the flight very slow. An ideal parachute flight goes down slowly and straight with no wobbling.

Wire Sculpture

Alexander Calder (1937) once said, "Wire, or something to twist, or tear, or bend, is an easier medium for me to think in" (p. 63). The linear aspects of wire invite sculptures reminiscent of line drawings. Whether attached to a base or hanging as a mobile, wire invites movement. Remind students that the ends of wire can be very sharp and to fold them over into their sculptures. While pipe cleaners are an excellent choice for young children, easy-to-bend wire can be easily used by primary students. Heavier gauge wire for older students requires professional tools, which are an incentive for this type of work. Consider borrowing safety goggles from the science department when using heavy gauge wire. As students gain familiarity with wire, they will find unexpected ways to decorate their sculptures with beads, buttons, sequins, and paper cutouts.

Papier Mâché

Papier mâché ties together many concepts learned throughout the year. With simple materials for armatures and inexpensive paste, students create anything from masks to animals to huge figures. Armatures made of recycled materials are carefully taped together. Name tags, color-coded by class, identify student work in the early stages. Storage can be a problem, so papier mâché might be offered as an ephemeral center for part of the school year. Stagger start times so the work will be at differing stages throughout the process.

Plaster

Plaster gauze, though more expensive than papier mâché, is much easier to store and has a lot of flexibility. Armatures can be created from newspaper, small boxes, cardboard, and wire, with a wooden base to stabilize the sculpture. For masks, cut gallon water containers in half. Students learn to set up their materials, cut pieces from the large roll of gauze, and make detailed three-dimensional artwork. Experienced students coach newcomers. Plaster can be painted while still damp and embellishments complete these sculptures.

TAKING WORK HOME OR LEAVING IT BEHIND

Many students new to sculpture will want to take their work home that very day, as they are extremely proud of their creations. Some teachers don't allow the option of stopping at construction and talk about painting or covering the sculpture with paper as the next step toward completion. When decorated, a student's sculpture might look more like a rocket ship and less like an oatmeal container with a pudding cup taped on top. Surface decoration allows the artist to fully realize the original vision. You will have to decide how finished the work must be before it goes home. There are arguments on both sides of this issue: some students may feel strongly that their work is finished and do not wish to add more. The excitement that they feel for sharing this work with their families is quite powerful. Others may be unaware of just how much further they can go with their work. This will adjust in time. As students become more familiar with the range of possibilities and offerings of materials, they are better equipped to make informed decisions. Plate 9.3 shows a work that progressed over many weeks' time at the sculpture center.

Prior to paint and decoration, cardboard sculptures often take several classes to complete. Some teachers are fortunate to have ample facilities to keep sculptures in the art room. If you do not, try working out an arrangement with classroom teachers for storage. Students who are obsessed with their work are likely to transport it back and forth from home. Intense preoccupation with work in progress is characteristic of focused artists. Remember that a goal of choice-based teaching and learning is to support the development of such artistic behaviors.

CHAPTER **10**

More Media Centers

A great deal of surprise is built into printmaking. Lifting the paper
off the printing surface is a tense and revelatory moment.
(Mazur, 1980, p. 57)

Drawing, painting, collage, and sculpture make up the basic studio centers
in a choice-based art program, but these media are insufficient to meet the
needs of all students. Three more studio centers—printmaking, clay, and fiber
arts—are discussed in this chapter. Together, these six centers are essential to
a comprehensive visual art experience. Depending upon your circumstances,
you may have separate areas for each of these media or include them within
larger studio centers.

Printmaking, clay and fiber arts, with their unique physical and tactile at-
tributes, appeal to a majority of students because these media and processes
are often unavailable at home. In recent years, opportunities for home studio
work have diminished with shifts in children's play from hands-on to technology. Enticing new materials motivate children to develop skills in unfamiliar
territory.

PRINTMAKING

Every time artists plan next steps they are Envisioning. Every time they step back
and ask themselves how the work would look if they made some kind of alteration
they are Envisioning.
(Hetland et al., 2007, p. 52)

Printmaking is the art of second chances. If the first print is unsuccessful,
print it again! Print and print and then save only the best! Printmaking is also
the art of the unexpected. Some students may be uncomfortable with the
many surprises inherent in printmaking. Others love the moment of pulling
the paper away from the printing plate to see what has happened. Printmak-

ing can be difficult to manage with large classes, but with multiple studio choices, you can work with a few interested students at a time.

Entry Into Printmaking

Early in the year, simple printmaking processes with stamps and foam are introduced. The following conversation illustrates one such introductory demonstration.

"What is a print?" a teacher asks the class.

Students think for a moment and hands go up. "A print is what you make on the computer when you can print your work."

"That's true," the teacher responds. "Can you make more than one print of your work?"

"Yes!" the children all respond enthusiastically.

"Can you make five copies? Ten copies? One hundred copies (if you are allowed to)?"

Squeals of laughter fill the air.

"Are all the copies exactly the same?" the teacher asks carefully.

A momentary pause and then children respond again "Yes."

"When you print here in the art room, you can also get many copies of the same thing. In art, we call these prints *multiples*. It is very similar to printing on your computer, except that each print is handmade."

The activities discussed here prepare students for more complex forms of printmaking and are easy to manage for young children.

Rubber Stamps. A table is set up with rubber stamps and several inkpads. The stamps are of geometric shapes. By combining these shapes, a wide range of designs and narrative art can be created. Students also incorporate collage materials with their stamp art and become aware of patterns, variations, and symmetry. Markers are available to add details. Plate 10.1 shows a child designing with shape stamps.

Quick Foam Prints. Markers are a convenient printing ink for foam plates, making it easy to start and finish in one day. Students draw on the foam surface with water-based markers. Next, paper is dampened on both sides with a sponge, placed over the printing plate, and pressed down. Through trial and error, students discover the best degree of paper wetness for their images. Encourage printers to make several versions of the same image to develop an understanding of multiples. This portable center is easy to cleanup and packs neatly into a shoebox.

Stenciling. Although not technically a printmaking process, stenciling is good practice for silkscreen printing and for making multiples. Paint daubers are useful for simple stenciling as well as designing and decorating. Students fold tag board in half, then cut on the fold to create a stencil shape. The paint dauber is tapped gently to fill up the opening in the stencil with a layer of paint, creating a positive shape. Patterns and overlapping create interesting stenciled designs.

Removable tape reinforces this concept. The tape is carefully laid down on good quality paper in a design. Markers, crayons and colored pencils can be used to completely color the paper. When the tape stencil is removed, areas of white paper are exposed; the edges are clean and sharp. The same pieces of tape are reused to overlap more layers of color. These designs take a bit of patience and are appropriate for Grades 3 and up.

Monoprints

A monoprint artist needs pigment, a printing plate, a tool to make the image, and a surface on which to print. Because the directions for monoprinting are not complex, these techniques are easy to incorporate into existing painting or printmaking centers. Plate 10.2 shows how to set up a small monoprint center. There are four variations for monoprinting:

1. *Folded paper monoprint.* Thick paper is folded in half, with one side of the paper taking the role of the plate and the other side the surface to be printed on. Using thick tempera paint, one color is brushed quickly onto one half of the paper, then the student folds and rubs. After the paper is opened, a second color can be added and the paper folded once again. Using one color at a time ensures that the earlier layers will dry so new colors retain their brilliance.

2. *Tempera monoprint.* Students paint on a large sheet of Plexiglas (the printing plate), changing and erasing their painting with a sponge. Working quickly is important so that the paint does not dry. Plastic sgraffito sticks as well as sponges can be used to scrape into the painted area. Paper is placed on the wet paint and a print is lifted.

3. *Fingerpaint on Plexiglas.* Students hold a piece of paper behind their back with one hand while fingerpainting on Plexiglass with the other, changing and erasing until they like their design. Their finger is the tool, and when they print and lift their paper they will notice that their image is reversed, an important thing to remember when printmaking.

4. *Brayers and ink.* Students ink the Plexiglas plate with brayers, scrape lines into it with tools, put paper down and rub. White ink on black paper and black ink on white paper show the best contrast. Dry prints can be colored with crayon, marker, or oil pastel.

Having multiple monoprint techniques available helps students see connections among the various types and internalize the big ideas of monoprinting. Students use menus to set up their monoprint materials throughout the year and are responsible for their own cleanup.

Relief Printmaking

Preparation of Styrofoam, collograph, and linoleum printing plates differs and is explained next. The process of inking remains the same for all three types of printmaking.

Foam Printing. Styrofoam sheets can provide a quick printmaking experience with just markers or become more involved when engraving the plate and printing with ink. For the latter, students draw first on paper, and then tape the paper to the foam surface. Tracing over the lines in a different color pencil allows the artist to see what he has already drawn, while transferring the idea from paper to the foam print. Once the basic concept is on the foam, the artist removes the paper to enhance the drawing directly on the foam surface, adding details.

Collographs. Collographs connect many collage concepts with printmaking. Designs are built on sturdy backgrounds, incorporating layers of shapes through overlaps and textures. Students need little assistance preparing their printing plates. It is helpful to place the printing plates under books separated with wax paper, so they dry flat. Printing is the same as for other relief processes, except that the collograph plate cannot be washed after printing!

Linoleum Printing. Many art teachers avoid linoleum printing because of safety issues. In the choice-based classroom you can supervise small groups of students as they use the sharp cutting tools and heat up the linoleum with an iron for easier cutting. If too many students are interested, set up several staggered teams. Limit the number of students who are printing at the same time to keep printing areas clean and organized.

Printing Relief Plates. In the busy choice-based art room keeping order is essential. Let students know that they will prepare the plate first and print during the following class when they have sufficient time to experiment with inks and brayers. For printing both foam and linoleum plates, set up separate areas for inking and printing and establish rules to keep paper free of fingerprints. Students will enjoy matching ink with various colors of paper and experimenting with the inking process. Printmaking is the art of multiples, so each artist is required to print the same image several times. Students compare variations in color, texture, and clarity in their finished prints.

Silkscreen

Silkscreen printing also benefits from small-group instruction. One table is set up with six small screens, six colors of finger paint, and six squeegees. Another table is set up with pencils and paper for printing. Use construction paper scraps to cut stencils. Students usually print only one color during the first class.

In the next class, all students print a second color following a review by the teacher. Students arrange new stencils to create overlaps when the second color is printed. Registration is not a problem. These are mostly abstract works; if the registration is slightly off, interesting edges are created. It is at this point that students begin to understand the process and the manipulation of positive and negative space. Children who continue with silkscreen printing gain a lot of control over what happens on their paper as they progress, cutting more stencils to add layers.

Embellishing Prints

Printmakers reflect on their work and may add more colors, paint or draw into the prints, or cut them up for collage. Plate 10.3 shows a young printmaker planning her next step. The most inviting is the occasional print which looks not so good or even terrible. With this print, the artist has nothing to lose. Some students use the paper trimmer to change the shape or to remove smudgy parts that they do not like. Others spice up the print with oil pastels or paint or chalk. Some of the most interesting prints are painted. Students who have been nervous about painting in the past may be very comfortable working paint into their unsatisfactory print. Wonderful images emerge! Manipulating prints after reflection helps students go deeper with printmaking.

CLAY STUDIO CENTER

I had something as a child that I lost. That capacity I lost made paper into a million things; things I could cut out, paste up, fold, tear, wrap, and fly. It made leaves into forests and the people in the books I read into close personal and private friends. As with many of the rest of you, this gift of being able to make images, to express wishes, to not as yet separate reality from fantasy, was educated out of me. But here we are back again, given a second and third chance to play with our clay in our own way.

(Berensohn, 1972, p. 90)

Nothing in the art room matches the magic of clay, with its tactile qualities and mysterious transformations in the kiln. When clay is first offered, children will be desperate for a turn right away. If you have enough tools and are willing to allow clay around the classroom, invite everyone to have a turn in the first week. It may require a little more management, but it is well worth the effort. After the first clay class, limit the number of students at the clay studio center. This will help to extend your clay supply throughout the year and keep the firing schedule manageable.

Kindergartners are asked, "Did you bring your clay tools with you today?" They raise their hands and wiggle their fingers to indicate that they are ready to form, pinch, squeeze, and shape their clay pieces. Very basic clay skills are introduced: rolling a ball, pinching out a hollow shape, rolling coils and attaching them, smoothing or erasing the separation between joined pieces and rolling a slab. The first day's demonstration focuses on containers and the second on sculptures such as animals, figures, planes, and shapes.

Kitchen gadgets from yard sales make excellent tools! Cover tables with muslin; the investment pays off at cleanup time. Cut clay into small cubes and place them in a plastic bag. A second bag holds clay scraps for students who need more. As numbers diminish at the clay center, you can offer larger amounts of clay.

Scoring and wedging are critical techniques for independent clay work. Without scoring clay pieces together, attachments fall off and accumulate at the bottom of the kiln. Combs or toothbrushes are good tools for scoring clay. Remind children to push firmly on attachments and smooth out the seams. Show learners how to wedge small pieces back together so they can continue with workable clay. Keep water handy as clay tends to dry out quickly. It is especially important to have a good system for labeling and returning clay artwork. Help students learn a routine for clearly labeling their work. Taking time to do this accurately now will save precious time later on. Plate 10.4 shows students taking responsibility for their clay work.

Clay, like paint, is a material that is not available to many students outside of school. They may need time to explore the clay by rolling, mashing, building, and tearing it apart. Some children may not have any desire to keep their experiments. Play dough or plasticine is a good material for this type of discovery learning. Other children may begin with an idea right away and seek out natural clay.

The teacher may not be a clay artist, but many students are. Experienced children enthusiastically coach their classmates in the many clay strategies they have discovered. One student announced that she would make a peacock with feathers spread. Speaking frankly about concerns that her piece would be too fragile to survive firing, her teacher tried to redirect her. Knowing the risks, the student persisted—with success. Another student formed a series of six clay angels in little shrines. These exquisite figures became increasingly detailed and more skillfully constructed with each attempt. The work of this

7-year-old student inspired others to create their own small figures, demonstrating similar artistic behaviors of perseverance and refinement.

Wheel throwing is an activity that is possible in a choice-based environment because all students can be actively engaged while several students take turns at the wheel, coaching each other. Photographs showing basic hand positions for throwing and opening forms help students learn proper techniques. Keep it simple so more students can explore this process.

FIBER ARTS CENTER

Anything that can be drawn, can be stitched. Fiber artists become enchanted with color, texture, and pattern. Yarns are arranged in palettes of wonderful colors and the artist is invited to choose those that connect to individual aims. Students enjoy making functional objects, often creating items for favorite toys or gifts for family members. Those who have difficulties with drawing or other two-dimensional work often excel when using yarn and cloth.

All of the work that students do with fiber is intentionally simple because beginners need to work independently. Once they master the skills of threading needles, knotting, and weaving, there is no limit to their direction in fiber arts.

Stitching

Stitching on Styrofoam is a great beginning for sewing, as it stays flat with no bunching up. Students are taught to thread big needles, double the yarn, and tie a knot at the end. These skills take practice! Children stitch in many colors and then decorate with markers. Some students sew two pieces together and this technique can double as an attachment strategy in the sculpture center.

Burlap is introduced next because the loose weave easily accepts plastic needles. Start with a simple activity, such as learning to sew a pocket. Show children how to sew a simple seam. Use the same needle-threading procedure as with Styrofoam, and stitch two pieces of burlap together with the running stitch or the backstitch. Some children sew pocketbooks and wallets, others sew little pouches or sleeping bags for their stuffed animals. With two pieces of burlap sewn on three sides, students can stuff cotton into the pocket, sew the fourth side, and make a pillow. Pillows may be embroidered or decorated with permanent markers.

Older students learn to sew fabric with needles and thread. The same pocket concept can be repeated with cotton and turned inside out, allowing endless possibilities! Rag dolls and soft sculptures of many sorts engage certain children. As learners gain understanding about knots and seams, their stitching repertoires will grow and flourish.

Weaving

Cardboard and box-lid looms are economical and allow children to decorate and keep the loom as part of their artwork if they choose. Plate 3.2 shows a loom warped with alternating colors, a strategy to simplify learning how to weave. Experienced weavers will want to warp their looms themselves. Weaving is a popular choice for students during bad weather as children can keep their weavings in their classrooms.

Open-Edge Weaving. Divide a box into twelve sections and fill each section with short pieces of yarn divided by color (i.e., several shades of red, several of orange, and so on). The yarn pieces are 2 inches longer than the cardboard is wide. Students choose colors and weave over and under, but allow the pieces to hang off the sides instead of looping around. Rows are pushed together with plastic combs serving as beaters. When children take their weaving off the loom, show them how to tie the warp threads together. More experienced children can try weaving with Egyptian knots and rya knots. As third grader Nick writes, the resulting pieces are very easy to make and look attractive:

> I have been weaving from first grade to third grade. It is fun. I look for different pieces of yarn, ribbon, and shoelace for my weavings. It's fun that way. Sometimes I mix thick yarn with thin yarn. I often use a pattern. This is a scarf for my mother and my nana. My nana sells scarves that she knits. Knitting frustrates me so I stick to weaving.

Tabby Weaving. In tabby weaving, weft threads are woven back and forth into the warp, leaving clean edges. Warp looms tightly with strong yarn. Students can wrap their weft yarn on small pieces of cardboard for a shuttle. Remind them to keep a "bubble" at each edge so the weaving does not pull inwards, causing the overall shape to distort. With practice, students will add variation in pattern, color, and design. Some enjoy inserting buttons, beads, feathers, and drawings into their weavings.

Stick Weavings. Even really young children can understand complex ideas. A simple technique such as stick weaving initiates a discussion of *symbolism*. Yarn is woven around two or more sticks tied together to form a cross. Students are invited to create their own symbolism for the colors they choose and the points of the sticks. Small children have no trouble doing this and their symbols relate to friends, family, pets, and sports teams. Later, the word *variation* is introduced and students are challenged to make a stick weaving unlike anyone else's. "What would happen if you used three sticks? Four? Sticks taped together in various configurations? Feathers, beads, and ribbon?" The simplest of art forms can carry deep meaning.

Art reflects the culture in which it was created. which includes the rich subculture of children. On a fall day, one kiln yielded baseballs, trophies, bats, caps (during the World Series), jack-o-lanterns, little laptops and cell phones, spaghetti with meatballs, pizza, racing cars, hearts, and tea sets. Weavings in orange and black join print images of turkeys and football games as evidence of the influence of children's visual culture on their artmaking. When teachers acknowledge and respect children's interests, students feel safe to take risks with their work and are able to grow as artists.

CHAPTER 11

Smaller and Ephemeral Centers

Engagement is the magnet that attracts learners' meandering attention
and holds it so that enduring learning can occur.
(Tomlinson, 1999, p. 38)

A choice-based classroom with painting, drawing, printing, fiber, collage, and sculpture centers can be quite complete, but some teachers find that additional small centers improve the arrangement and provide inspiration to students. If space is a problem, the ideas and materials in these minicenters can be folded into existing centers. You can also assemble "centers-in-a-box." Even small centers contain menus, visual resources, and tools along with limited quantities of materials.

Ephemeral centers hold media that make a brief appearance in the art room just once during the school year. Factors in the decision to make a studio center ephemeral include messy or complicated processes, materials in short supply, and space. Sometimes ephemeral centers can meet requirements of the district curriculum or satisfy a child's curiosity about a particular art process. Examples of centers that some choice-based teachers choose to make ephemeral are papermaking and marbling, mosaics, soapstone carving, sumi ink painting, papier mâché and sand casting. Teachers have an affinity for certain media; what is ephemeral in one classroom may be a basic studio center in another. Any of the following centers may be either ephemeral or arranged as a small studio center, depending upon preference and need.

BOOK ARTS

Altered Books

What happens when a printed book becomes an art object? Someone has discarded books and student artists transform them to create something extraordinary. Altered book artists work with paint, oil pastels, markers, magazines, rubber stamps, and other basic materials. Remind students using paint and glue that each page spread must lie open to dry. Books can be stored together by class. This is very useful for art teachers working from a cart as altered books, like weavings, can be stored in classrooms and are always available. Ask your librarian to save damaged and undesirable books. A library lesson can be integrated on the care of good books.

Simple Books

Offer bookbinding strategies that your students can use without teacher support. The simplest is stapling down one side of a book. Students should complete their pages before stapling them together. Otherwise, you will see many pieces of blank drawing paper go out the door, probably never to be used. Limit the number of pages to four, plus covers. When students demonstrate that they can handle more pages, extend the limit two pages at a time.

Small books are very popular and index cards are a good size. Students can use a two-hole office punch to prepare for bindings. Paper fasteners can bind these small books together. An attractive method is to push each end of an elastic band through the two holes and then insert a craft stick or dowel through the protruding elastic loops, holding them in place. Leave a box of small paper, punches, markers, scissors, craft sticks, and elastics at the book arts center.

DIGITAL ART

The computer is an encyclopedia, a typewriter, a post office, a darkroom, and enticing equipment for artmaking. Many children are familiar with basic art programs. Some digital art centers have electronic tablets with pens, but students can draw with the mouse. Digital photography allows young children to pause and study their world through the camera lens. The immediacy of this art form engages the youngest of students and provides them with a valuable life skill. Simple photo editing programs invite students to manipulate their photos, while learning about important concepts such as light and contrast.

For some children, digital art serves a need not filled by other media. The ability to flood colors in a background or to erase repeatedly helps students experience remarkable success. Jack is a fifth-grade student who is devoted to digital art and shares his wealth of knowledge with both classmates and teachers:

My grandfather had Mac Classic and that was my first computer when I was in preschool. The first thing I learned was how to make a picture with MacPaint. Then I learned how to type and make words. I sat there day after day trying to learn how to do things. With computers, you can make art a lot faster. If you don't like it, it didn't take 5 days to draw so you can just undo it and change it to something you like better. Digital cameras give you a better chance of getting a picture of something that might otherwise escape.

Older students can use simple programs including PowerPoint for drawn animation and digital cameras for stop-motion clips. Even if a printer is not readily available, teach students how to set up folders to store their work. Photo editing in iPhoto or Photoshop invites innovative behaviors and further exploration. A digital art gallery of student work will inspire more artists to explore this studio center.

MASK MAKING

Masks intrigue children! The teacher talks about the essence of masks. "Masks can scare you or make you laugh, masks are beautiful or ugly, masks are realistic or fantastic, masks can be people or animals or something else! Masks are used to celebrate holidays, tell stories, or as a costume or uniform. Masks hide you or tell people about you. What sort of mask will you make?"

Students start with paper masks that can be embellished with materials from various centers. Visual references include multicultural masks, theater and holiday masks, and masks used in sports and jobs. The vocabulary word *exaggerate* encourages artists to go the extra mile. *Transformation* is another good term as the artist transforms a piece of paper, and the artist, too, is transformed. Chris, a third grader, really looked forward to the opening of the mask center. His initial idea for a mask led him to specialize in protruding forms:

Masks are the best things I do in art. I am really good at doing horns. I taught a lot of other people how to make horns on their masks.

Plastic forms make good bases for papier mâché or plaster masks. If these are not available, use gallon water jugs cut in half. Students cover the form with layers of papier mâché or plaster gauze. When the base is dry, features made of aluminum foil are attached and covered. Students are encouraged to consider facial expressions as they work. In subsequent weeks, students paint

---

Sidebar 11.1. Murals

The mural center is easy to set up. I tack a 7 x 3 foot piece of bulletin board paper on a stiff piece of compressed cardboard and lean it on the wall. Our kids really get into it. We start with crayons, markers, and colored pencils, then India ink. We add tempera paint and collage. So far I have about 15 completed murals rolled up in the back storage room. I will get them out at some point and have students rework them. I might even connect them all together and construct a megamural. If I don't have a new piece of mural paper at the center when a new class enters the room, the muralists will remind me! "Hey, Mr. Gaw! When are you going to put up a new mural paper? We want to work on murals today!" Later, we will do some follow-up discussion and dialogue about mural artists and history. But right now, they are busy in the production phase. I have observed that a large percentage of children are drawn to that center. There is something aesthetically appealing for them to work so big.

—Clyde Gaw (2005)

---

and decorate their masks. Peer coaching and manageable numbers make this center easy to maintain.

PUPPET CENTER

Puppets are magical to children. Simple puppet bodies from tubes, sticks, paper bags, and boxes are introduced by the teacher. Materials for embellishing the puppets are available, as shown in Plate 11.1. To avoid multiple quickly constructed puppets, students are expected to know their puppet's personality. When they show off their character, ask them to tell you who it *really is*. Encourage students to make homes, cars, and meals for their puppets. There is no one more intent than a child in chosen play. Teaching for artistic behavior leverages play as a valuable learning opportunity.

Some art rooms have space for a puppet theatre during all or part of the year. Students may show skill at playwriting and others will improvise their stories. If possible, allow time for occasional puppet performances in the classroom. To keep it fair and positive, here are rules written by students:

1. Four puppeteers at a time. Sign up to join a group.
2. Ten-minute sessions unless no one else is waiting.
3. Puppets cannot do anything that students cannot do at school: *No yelling, no hitting, no biting.*

4. Audience sits behind the taped line (3 feet from stage).
5. Laughter and applause are appreciated.
6. Directing, calling out, and negative comments from the audience are not allowed.

ARCHITECTURE

In the architecture center, students design buildings using blocks. Conversations focus on what architects do. Reference materials about architects, forms, and vocabulary join simple photos and diagrams. Students working there know where their building is sited (city, country, beach) and its purpose (school, apartment, fort). This may seem overly simple, but many young students have never heard the word *architecture* before. Blocks are used to build structures. Digital photographs of students' structures make young architects more comfortable with taking apart their work. Magnetic architectural shapes facilitate designs that can be photocopied to bring home.

Teaching for artistic behavior necessitates adapting the learning environment to modify behaviors. Small and ephemeral centers energize the art room and capture students who may not have connected with a favorite medium yet. The thrill of new choices activates fresh ideas, behaviors and thinking. Certain ephemeral centers appear at the same time each year and children excitedly anticipate their arrival. Ephemeral centers may motivate learners who are looking for more focused, short-term activities. It is a satisfying feeling to find creative ways of differentiation so all students can be successful.

CHAPTER 12

Rethinking Art Education

Postmodernism challenges educators to explore a worldview that envisions schooling through a different lens of indeterminancy, aesthetics, autobiography, intuition, eclecticism, and mystery. In this sense, a concrete definition of postmodern education with universal goals, behavioral objectives, and predetermined outcomes is an oxymoron.

(Slattery, 1995, p. 23)

Students' learning styles, interests, and play habits reflect changes in society over the past 40 years. Postmodern education acknowledges the impact of these changes by addressing the need for personal relevancy in teaching and learning, and remaining open to possibilities. Flexibility, comfort with ambiguity, and the constant reconceptualizing of what a curriculum is and should be calls for reimagining the field of education.

Visual art education has the unique opportunity to promote learner-directed experiences without compromising the content of the discipline. Unlike orchestral music, for example, there is no reason that every artist must be performing at the same place and at the same time. Art teachers can reexamine the whys and hows of their pedagogy to see if they are really challenging their students. Mimicry does not ensure understanding. Nor does it respect students' abilities to develop and pursue their own ideas through planning, collaboration, innovation, and reflection. The teacher who is always in control of every aspect of teaching and learning may never see what is truly important in the lives of children.

From the child's point of view, this pedagogy is simple and direct and allows the pursuit of complex ideas with autonomy. However, choice-based teaching and learning is a challenging practice for new and veteran teachers alike. In order to provide for independent learning, the instructor must be organized, flexible, and responsive to a variety of concerns. Emergent curriculum requires constant tweaking and improvement, often with the help of student input. What worked well one year might not be useful over time because other, more relevant topics come up in later years.

The practice of choice-based art education originated in the school setting. A strong case has been made for this pedagogical philosophy as an essential foundation for teaching and learning in the visual arts. The genuine challenge of meeting the needs of all learners combined with the physical issues of time, space, and materials are realities often disregarded in even the best educational theory. This disconnect between theory and practice is evident when researchers distance themselves from the real world of schools. In recent years the philosophy of teaching for artistic behavior has been refined through action research conducted by hundreds of practicing teachers each day in their classrooms. We challenge readers to continue questioning the practice and to share their findings in professional learning communities. Among the many possibilities for study, we wonder about the following:

- Are there commonalities between school art and home art? How does one support the other?
- What is most useful for teachers to know about childrens' understandings and how can that best be evidenced in assessment practices?
- What effect do teacher interests and preferences have on the choices students make?
- What major themes emerge in independent student work and what is the relationship between these themes and visual culture? How do these themes change as students mature?
- How can art teachers collaborate with special education teachers to meet the needs of students? How can the teaching for artistic behavior philosophy support these students in other areas of their learning?
- Are there gender differences in the choices students make?
- How do students' attitudes toward their artmaking change as they move from grade to grade and school to school?
- What do the dynamics of self-selected student collaboration look like? What are the outcomes for students in art class, general education, and outside of school?

Why do we teach art? Is it to encourage children to experience the joys and struggles of authentic personal studio work similar to that of practicing artists? Is it to teach the mechanics of visual art so the learner gains a working knowledge of media and techniques? Is it to expose children to important history surrounding the arts and give them a context for the work they are doing? If curriculum is to contain all of these components and be meaningful, then the structure of art class needs to change. In a learner-directed classroom, children are not passive; teachers hold high standards for them and they have broad responsibilities. In particular, students are held accountable for their decisions regarding their work because they have the opportunity to *choose* what they do and how they do it. If we wish for our students to do the work of artists, we must offer them the opportunity to behave as artists, think as artists, and perform as artists. If not in art classrooms, then where?

National Visual Art Standards

What Fourth Graders in Teaching for Artistic Behavior Art Programs Know and Can Do

Content Standard 1: Understanding and applying media, techniques, and processes

Achievement Standard:

- Students know the differences between materials, techniques, and processes.
- Students describe how different materials, techniques, and processes cause different responses.
- Students use different media, techniques, and processes to communicate ideas, experiences, and stories.
- Students use art materials and tools in a safe and responsible manner.

When students are permitted to explore materials of their choosing, they learn about unique properties through authentic experiences. Children in choice-based art programs apply this knowledge to make decisions about the best media to express their ideas, developing artistic behaviors and techniques that become part of their unique creative process.

Content Standard 2: Using knowledge of structures and functions

Achievement Standard:

- Students know the differences among visual characteristics and purposes of art in order to convey ideas.
- Students describe how different expressive features and organizational principles cause different responses.
- Students use visual structures and functions of art to communicate ideas.

Structures and functions provide a descriptive framework for planning, executing, and responding to visual art. In the context of learner-directed work, elements and principles emerge and become embedded in student understandings.

Content Standard 3: Choosing and evaluating a range of subject matter, symbols, and ideas

Achievement Standard:

- Students explore and understand prospective content for works of art.
- Students select and use subject matter, symbols, and ideas to communicate meaning.

In choice-based teaching and learning, students are adept at making real choices in both materials and subject matter. Learner-directed artmaking results in work that reflects the beliefs and values of the artist.

Content Standard 4: Understanding the visual arts in relation to history and cultures

Achievement Standard:

- Students know that the visual arts have both a history and specific relationships to various cultures.
- Students identify specific works of art as belonging to particular cultures, times, and places.
- Students demonstrate how history, culture, and the visual arts can influence each other in making and studying works of art.

Teaching for artistic behavior exposes students to a wide variety of contemporary and historical artworks in both formal and informal discussions. Students find connections between their own work and that of established artists. Children make personal connections with the work of accomplished artists, becoming familiar with a wide range of styles and influences.

Content Standard 5: Reflecting upon and assessing the characteristics and merits of their work and the work of others

Achievement Standard:

- Students understand that there are various purposes for creating works of visual art.
- Students describe how people's experiences influence the development of specific artworks.
- Students understand that there are different responses to specific artworks.

Self-assessment is a valued component of teaching for artistic behavior. Students engage in discussions about their artistic intentions, maintain journals, analyze their own work and that of other artists. Through this reflective process, students become cognizant of how they can communicate ideas through art.

Content Standard 6: Making connections between visual arts and other disciplines

Achievement Standard:

- Students understand and use similarities and differences between characteristics of the visual arts and other arts disciplines.
- Students identify connections between the visual arts and other disciplines in the curriculum.

Students communicate their interests through artmaking. These interests frequently include topics discussed in other classes. In this manner, students integrate knowledge from other disciplines into their artwork.

Written Planning for the Choice-Based Teacher

Teaching for artistic behavior is not meant to be a formula. This lesson plan reflects the organic nature of a choice-based classroom, offering direction in the structuring of lessons. Lessons are not taught in their entirety at the beginning of class, or throughout one class, or even in consecutive weeks. Teachers consider everything they might want children to know about a topic or material and then focus on what is the *least* they can say to get students working productively. Core concepts become the demonstration, a 5-minute introduction at the beginning of class. Once students are working, the teacher observes and decides what else is needed, using direct or indirect instruction. Historical references, anecdotes, and relevant concepts surface through discussions with individual students or the entire class where appropriate.

The following provides a model for structuring written lesson plans. Use it as a reference, modify it, and write your own, adding what you need to address the needs of your students, school, and district.

INTRODUCTION TO THE COLLAGE CENTER: GRADES 1 AND 2—ADAPTABLE FOR ALL GRADES

Objectives

Students will:

- Develop basic skills, techniques, tool usage, and safety, enabling independent work
- Collect shapes, pictures, colored paper, and textures
- Interpret their art ideas using cut-paper collage
- Use appropriate vocabulary to discuss their artwork

Concepts

- Make a collage by gluing two-dimensional materials to a surface, creating one cohesive image
- Arrange and rearrange layers and materials
- Overlap to create layers
- Vary line quality by cutting and tearing different edges on shapes

Art History References

- Pablo Picasso
- Henri Matisse
- Romare Beardon

Supplies and Equipment

Tools and materials: Straight and fancy-edge scissors, glue, glue sticks, brass fasteners, punches, paper trimmer

Collections of collage materials: Construction paper, scrap paper, recycled cut letters from bulletin boards, magazines, recycled wrapping paper, wallpaper samples, shiny materials, ribbons, fibers, and whatever else your students collect

Demonstration (5–8 minutes)

Dialogue: "Today we are going to open a new center, the Collage Center. This is where you will create artwork by cutting, arranging, and gluing paper shapes. Take one sheet of paper as your base. *Find* shapes, pictures, colors, or textures. Cut or tear shapes of paper or use shapes you find. Different *edges* make your collage more interesting. *Arrange* your shapes on the paper, look at them, and decide if that's how you want them. *Rearrange* them if you want. Some of your shapes might *overlap*. *Glue* the large pieces first and then layer smaller pieces on top."

Studio Time

Students make one or more collages using their own ideas. As always, students can choose this art form or make art in any way they like that has been previously demonstrated. Students who choose collage will be directed to remember the concepts discussed in the demo. The teacher moves about and encourages students, pointing out great discoveries to the class. Individual direction is provided for the kind of collage each student is making. References to historical content are made as opportunities arise. Five minutes before cleanup, students should glue down their remaining pieces or gather them into a stapled paper folder.

Cleanup

Dialogue: "Put away all tools and pick up all loose bits of paper from the table and floor. Put all usable scraps back in the appropriate boxes, put boxes on the shelf, and throw away unusable scraps. An unusable scrap is one that is very small, or crinkled. This is how you will always cleanup at the Collage Center."

Assessment and Reflection

As time permits, use any of the following strategies to encourage reflection:

- Artists ask a classmate, "What did you make today?"
- "Who learned something in the Collage Center today? What did you learn?"
- "Who has some advice for the children who didn't choose collage today?"
- "Who would like to share artwork with the class?"
- "Are there any questions or comments about this artwork?"

Frameworks

This lesson supports the following National Visual Art Standards, which can be adapted to support your local or state frameworks:

Content Standard 1: Understanding and applying media, techniques, and processes
Content Standard 3: Choosing and evaluating a range of subject matter, symbols, and ideas
Content Standard 5: Reflecting upon and assessing the characteristics and merits of their work and the work of others

NOTE

Appendix B is reprinted with permission from Laurie Anderson Jakubiak (2005).

References

Amabile, T. M. (1996). *Creativity in context.* Boulder, CO: Westview Press.

Andrews, B. H. (2005). Art, reflection, and creativity in the classroom: The student-driven art course. *Art Education, 58*(4), 35–41.

Bayles, D. & Orland, T. (1993). *Art and fear: Observations on the perils (and rewards) of artmaking.* Santa Cruz, CA: The Image Continuum.

Beghetto, R. A. & Plucker, J. A. (2006). The relationship among schooling, learning, and creativity. In J. C. Kaufman & J. Baer (Eds.), *Creativity and reason in cognitive development* (pp. 316–332). New York: Cambridge University Press.

Berensohn, P. (1972). *Finding one's way with clay.* Dallas, TX: Biscuit Books.

Brooks, J., & Brooks, M. (1993). *In search of understanding: The case for constructivist classrooms.* Alexandria, VA: Association for Supervision and Curriculum Development.

Burton, D., & McGraw, T. (2001). Students as curators. In B. Zuk & R. Dalton (Eds.), *Student art exhibitions: New ideas and approaches.* Reston, VA: National Art Education Association.

Calder, A. (1937). Mobiles. In M. Evans (Ed.), *The painter's object* (pp. 63–67). London: Gerald Howe.

Calkins, L. M. (1994). *The art of teaching writing.* Portsmouth, NH: Heinemann.

Clark, R. (1996). *Art education issues in postmodernist pedagogy.* Reston, VA: National Art Education Association.

Crowe, J. (2002a). A conversation about choice-based art education: Why is it so effective? *Knowledgeloom.* Retrieved December 29, 2008 from http://knowledgeloom.org/tab/tab_transcript.html

Crowe, J. (2002b). Burnell laboratory school. *Knowledgeloom.* Retrieved December 29, 2008 from http://knowledgeloom.org/practice_story.jsp?t=1&bpid=1361&storyid=1227&aspect=2&location=3&parentid=1357&bpinterid=1357&spotlightid=1357

Douglas, K. (2004). *Kid culture.* Unpublished manuscript.

Douglas, K., Crowe, J., Jaquith, D., & Brannigan, R. (2002). Promising practices for a choice-based approach to art education. *Knowledgeloom.* Retrieved August 15, 2005, from http://knowledgeloom.org/practices3.jsp?location=1&bprinterid=1357&spotlightid=1357

Duckworth, E. (1996). *"The having of wonderful ideas" and other essays on teaching and learning.* New York: Teachers College Press.

Efland, A. (1976). The school art style: A functional analysis. *Studies in Art Education, 17*(3), 37–44.

Efland, A. (1990). *A history of art education: Intellectual and social currents in teaching the visual arts.* New York: Teachers College Press.

Efland, A., Freedman, K., Stuhr, P. (1996). *Postmodern art education: An approach to curriculum.* Reston, VA: National Art Education Association.

Eisner, E. (2002). *The arts and the creation of mind.* New Haven: Yale University Press.

Fasco, D., Jr. (2006). Creative thinking and reasoning: Can you have one without the other? In J. C. Kaufman & J. Baer (Eds.), *Creativity and reason in cognitive development* (pp. 159–176). New York: Cambridge University Press.

Fralick, C. (2007). *Curriculum mapping.* Unpublished manuscript.

Gaw, C. (2007). *Electronic portfolios.* Unpublished manuscript.

Gaw, C. (2005). *Murals.* Unpublished manuscript.

Gude, O. (2004). Postmodern principles: In search of a twenty-first century art education. *Art Education, 57*(1), 6–14.

Haring, K. (1996). *Keith Haring journals.* New York: Penguin Books.

Hathaway, N. (2005). *Resources for learning.* Unpublished manuscript.

Hathaway, N. (2006a). Is there a scribble stage for sculpture? *School Arts, 106*(4), 38–39.

Hathaway, N. (2006b). *Progress report.* Unpublished manuscript.

Hetland, L., Winner, E., Veenema, S., & Sheridan, K. (2007). *Studio thinking: The real benefits of visual arts education.* New York: Teachers College Press.

Hutchens, J., & Suggs, M. (Eds.). (1997). *Art education: Content and practice in a postmodern era.* Reston, VA: National Art Education Association.

Jacobs, H. H. (2004.) *Getting results with curriculum mapping.* Alexandria, VA: Association for Supervision and Curriculum Development.

Jakubiak, L. A. (2005). Unpublished manuscript. Boston, MA: Massachusetts College of Art.

Kandinsky, W. (1964). Reminiscences. In R. Herbert (Ed.), *Modern artists on art* (pp. 19–44). Englewood Cliffs, NJ: Prentice-Hall.

Lin, M. (2000). *Boundaries.* New York: Simon & Schuster.

London, P. (1989). *No more secondhand art: Awakening the artist within.* Boston: Shambhala.

Lowenfeld, V., & Brittain, W. (1957). *Creative and mental growth.* New York: Macmillan.

Mazur, M. (1980). *The painterly print: Monotypes from the seventeenth to the twentieth century.* New York: Metropolitan Museum of Art.

Moore, H. (1986). *Henry Moore: My ideas, inspiration and life as an artist.* London: Collins & Brown.

Muir, B. (2004, September 24). Curriculum night [msg. 538]. http://groups/yahoo.com/group/TAB-ChoiceArtEd/message/538

Ray, K. W. (2002). *What you know by heart.* Portsmouth, NH: Heinemann.

Runco, M. A. (2006). Reasoning and personal creativity. In J. C. Kaufman & J. Baer (Eds.), *Creativity and reason in cognitive development* (pp. 9–116). New York: Cambridge University Press.

Runco, Mark A. (2007). *Creativity theories and themes: Research, development, and practice*. Burlington, MA: Elsevier Academic Press.

Saphier, J., & Gower, R. (1997). *The skillful teacher: Building your teaching skills*. Acton, MA: Research for Better Teaching.

Slattery, P. (1995). *Curriculum development in the postmodern era*. New York: Garland.

Smith, P. (1995). Art and irrelevance. *Studies in Art Education, 36*(2), 123–125.

Smith, P. (1996). *The history of American art education: Learning about art in American schools*. Westport, CT: Greenwood Press.

Szekely, G. (1988). *Encouraging creativity in art lessons*. New York: Teachers College Press.

Szekely, G. (2005). Teaching students to become independent artists: A film script. *Art education, 58*(1), 41–51.

Thiebaud, W. (2000). In S. A. Nash & A. Gopnik, (Authors). *Wayne Thiebaud: A paintings retrospective*. San Francisco: Fine Arts Museums of San Francisco.

Tomlinson, C. (1999). *The differentiated classroom: Responding to the needs of all learners*. Alexandria, VA: Association for Supervision and Curriculum Development.

Tomlinson, C. (2001). *How to differentiate instruction in mixed-ability classrooms*. Alexandria, VA: Association for Supervision and Curriculum Development.

Topal, C. W., & Gandini, L. (1999). *Beautiful stuff: Learning with found materials*. Worcester, MA: Davis.

Index

About the Authors

Katherine M. Douglas has a B.S. in education from the University of Maryland and a master's degree in Integrated Studies from Cambridge College. She studied with Dr. Peter London in the Drawing From Within Institute and at the Massachusetts College of Art and Design Artist/Teacher Institute. After retiring from 36 years of teaching elementary art in Montgomery County, Maryland and East Bridgewater Massachusetts, Douglas has been a visiting lecturer at the Massachusetts College of Art and Design and an instructor at Stonehill College in Easton, Massachusetts. She has collaborated in international online educational projects using technology to connect teachers and students. Douglas was named Massachusetts Distinguished Art Teacher in 2005.

Diane B. Jaquith is a graduate of Bates College, with a major in fine arts, and has a master's degree in art education from the Massachusetts College of Art and Design. A K–12 educator, Jaquith currently teaches elementary art in Newton, Massachusetts, where she has run a choice-based art program for many years. Her teaching career began in museum education with adult classes at the Museum of Fine Arts, Boston, and working as a researcher for VUE, developers of Visual Thinking Strategies. Jaquith is a frequent presenter at state and national art education conferences and is the recipient of an NEA Foundation Award for Teaching Excellence in 2008.

Together, Douglas and Jaquith are cofounders (with John Crowe and Pauline Joseph) of Teaching for Artistic Behavior, Inc., an educational organization that supports teachers who practice choice-based art education. They are principal content providers for http://www.teachingforartisticbehavior.org, http://knowledgeloom.org/tab, and comoderate an art education listserv.